About the Author

Gareth Maher is an award-winning former journalist who is now Communications Manager with the Football Association of Ireland. A media officer at five different UEFA European Championships, he designed the award-winning National Football Exhibition and has spent his career promoting Irish football. He was the ghostwriter on Clare Shine's *Scoring Goals in the Dark (2022)*.

AWAY DAYS
First published in 2022 by
New Island Books
Glenshesk House
10 Richview Office Park
Clonskeagh
Dublin D14 V8C4
Republic of Ireland
www.newisland.ie

Print ISBN: 978-1-84840-869-2
eBook ISBN: 978-1-84840-870-8

Set in 11.5 on 17pt Adobe Garamond Pro and 11.5 on 17pt and 30 on 36pt Alternate Gothic No 2.

Edited by Noel O'Regan
Cover design by Niall McCormack, hitone.ie
Cover images credits: Niall Quinn, Sunderland v Chelsea, PA Images/Alamy Stock Photo; John O'Shea, Manchester United, Jason Cairnduff/Action Images/REUTERS/Alamy Stock Photo; Seamus Coleman, Everton, Darren Staples/Sportimage/Alamy Stock Photo.
Typeset by JVR Creative India
Printed by ScandBook, Sweden, scandbook.com

New Island Books is a member of Publishing Ireland.

10 9 8 7 6 5 4 3 2 1

AWAY DAYS

GARETH MAHER

AWAY DAYS

Thirty Years of Irish Footballers in the Premier League

NEW ISLAND

Contents

Introduction

It is often advised not to meet your heroes for fear of being disappointed. Perhaps the failure, though, is understanding who the real heroes in our lives are. For me, it has always been, and always will be, my dad.

Sure, I had posters of my favourite footballers plastered over my bedroom walls and stacks of books by the writers who have inspired me. And I've been lucky enough to meet a lot of those people. But none compares to the one man who has been my most trusted counsellor, coach and confidant.

My dad never played football for a team yet he is by far the most intelligent observer, analyst and commentator on the game that I have yet to come across. He sees things differently, always has, and that enables him to simplify things in a world that can at times get caught up in trying too hard to impress. Dad calls it how he sees it and he is rarely wrong in his assessment – but never in a boastful way.

It is quite amazing that the person who, I feel, knows more about football than the hundreds of players, coaches, managers and analysts I've worked with is someone who is selft-taught and never played the game. That is the beauty of football; it can be interpreted and consumed in so many different ways.

When the Premiership first launched in 1992, it was like a circus had rolled into town. It was loud, colourful, packed with foreign attractions and thoroughly entertaining. I was hooked immediately. Except I didn't have a club to support. My brother, Mark, didn't want me lurking in his shadow so Liverpool was out of the question, while everyone else seemed to be Manchester United nuts. I didn't fancy following the crowd so I needed to find another club and eventually landed with Arsenal.

It would be some years later before I would become besotted with the League of Ireland, but you never forget your first love and that was the Premier League. I can remember swapping stickers with friends in the schoolyard, playing out on the street until daylight expired and Dad whistled to signal time was up, flicking through *Match* and *Shoot* magazines, learning everything that I could about every player at every club and watching all the live games, no matter who was playing.

When my brother brought me to Highbury for the first time, I felt like I was in the original version of *Fever Pitch*. The atmosphere was incredible. I became even more obsessed with football. And I started to write about it at every opportunity. In fact, I won a writing competition in primary school for a short story on it and my prize was a book by Alan Shearer on how to take penalty kicks. I cheekily asked my teacher, Mr Barry, if he could find one by Ian Wright instead!

I wasn't good enough to play football at a professional level but that never diluted my love of the game. If anything, it empowered it. The old saying is that if you can't play, you coach and if you can't coach you talk / write about it. I was comfortable with option three – even though I did dabble in coaching by earning my UEFA B Licence – and it was something that I made my career from; first in journalism and then working with the Football Association of Ireland.

Working in football has allowed me to meet some truly amazing people. Countless numbers of players, coaches and managers – male and female – have been fantastic in sharing their experiences and knowledge. Work colleagues, such as Stephen Finn, Darragh McGinley and the late Michael Hayes, are people who I could never tire speaking with about football. My brother remains my chief rival in footballing debates and I'm sure my nephew, Luke, will follow in his footsteps. But nobody beats Dad – he is the one who has always stirred up my passion for football.

I'm incredibly fortunate to have had parents who were always hugely encouraging of my two great hobbies: football and writing. Without their support, I would never have got to this stage of writing my first book and being able to shine a light on the Irish players who have made an impact on the Premier League in its first three decades.

This is a book about players and their stories. This is a book about the Premier League. This is a book about Irishmen defying the odds. But most of all, this is a book about falling in love with football.

Gareth Maher
October 2022

1

Niall Quinn

Manchester City (1992–96), Sunderland (1996–97, 1999–2003)
Games Played: 250
Goals Scored: 59
Assists Created: 37
Clean Sheets: 32
Yellow Cards: 26
Red Cards: 1
Wins: 79
Draws: 75
Losses: 96

The revolution will be televised.

Niall Quinn has had inside access to the Premier League on the pitch as a player, in the boardroom as a chairman and in the studio as a media pundit. So when he speaks about the league evolving into one of the world's most popular brands, he is worth listening to.

When Quinn first left his home in Dublin to join Arsenal in 1983, TV coverage of football consisted of a *Match of the Day* highlights package on Saturday nights and live broadcast of international games and the FA Cup Final. It was very seldom that a league game would be live on TV. English football was stuck in its traditional ways and being left behind by other European nations who were giving more access to TV broadcasters and tinkering their match schedules to suit their target audience. Something needed to be done to elevate the home of English football back to the top of the popularity polls. That is when the concept of a new top tier, named the Premiership, was first mooted.

From the 1992 season onwards, this new division would represent a fresh approach for English football. It would embrace a step away from the regular Saturday afternoon slot with games set to be spread out over a weekend on Sundays and even Monday nights. Many doubted whether this would be successful, but it was exactly this type of move that had seen American football take over as the dominant sport in the United States.

Years later, Quinn got to understand the Premier League's strategy when attending monthly stakeholder meetings in his role as Sunderland chairman. He was able to see how television played a significant part in the league's rise as a global brand. Not that it was all straightforward.

'I learned that it was very hard to get things done in the Premier League because the clubs kept fighting with each other. It was only when they appointed independent executives, who were not linked to any club, that real progress started to happen and they brought their brand around the world. They also had a partner who knew how this thing worked in America. Sky Sports are always either credited or discredited with bringing the Premier League to where it is, depending on how you look at it. Their owner at the time, Rupert Murdoch, had been all through this before in America and saw how it went into everyone's living rooms, into every pub and bar. So they followed a well-worn path of how it was done in American sports and Sky backed it. Then suddenly it was all in our faces.

'The interesting thing is that the matches are the matches, but to put a live feed out twenty-four hours a day about news on football was a huge move. When you think about it, that was a masterstroke. Funnily enough, when I look back at the Irish guys who took on Sky with Setanta Sports, one of the things I felt that they were slow in incorporating was a news feed. By the time they got it up, Sky were ahead of them with reporters outside training grounds and they almost became part of the furniture. One of the key things early on was that there was a feeling amongst the players that Sky were in this to promote it in the best possible light. There was no sense that they were out to do you. And that's interesting when you look at what way it has gone in recent times with pundits being quite critical of certain players, like Roy [Keane] was on Harry Maguire, for example.'

Still, the Premier League's embrace of commercialisation through maximising their TV coverage has clearly worked – to the extent that they could boast a global audience of 4.7 billion people as of 2022. The top other leagues around the world wanted to follow suit and still do. The likes of Serie A (Italy), La Liga (Spain), Bundesliga (Germany), Ligue 1 (France), Primeira Liga (Portugal), Eredivisie (Netherlands), Super Lig (Turkey), J League (Japan), Chinese Super League (China), Major League Soccer (United States) and Liga Apertura (Mexico) are all chasing the Premier League for a share of that TV audience.

Granting rights to broadcast games was one thing at the beginning of the 'Premiership' era, however; the next was ensuring that the TV companies had exclusive access to managers and players. This was a game-changer in how players would be treated as part of this TV revolution. It was no longer a case of asking nicely for a post-match interview with a jubilant player; instead, designated slots were assigned for pre- and post-match interviews. Failure to comply would result in a heavy fine.

Quinn explains: 'It was a big change to be told by your club that you have to do interviews. If you say that you didn't want to do interviews, they would say that you signed a contract and you have to do them. They muscled in on the players' contracts in theory, but it was all for the showbusiness.'

Once the TV companies had the live rights and the manager/player access, what they needed next was a slick marketing campaign. Sky Sports led the way with the tagline, 'It's a whole new ball game', using one player from each of the twenty-two clubs (Middlesbrough defender Alan

Kernaghan was the sole Irish player in there) in a TV advert that had 'Alive and Kicking' by Simple Minds as its soundtrack. This was more MTV than ITV, a bold new approach. 'It had gone like Hollywood, the players were like movie stars,' says Quinn.

Having joined Manchester City from Arsenal in 1992, Quinn was right in the middle of this new Premiership era as one of its main strikers. He saw how people were sucked in by the marketing, as if Sky had switched on a tractor beam that brought a whole new audience to the top division in English football. And if the marketing was hyped up enough, it could convince people of almost anything – or so Quinn suggests. 'The power of marketing and the power of looking at football differently to the modern fan and how their perception of football has changed is summed up by Georgi Kinkladze. He played for Man City for three years and won [the club's] Player of the Century! We were relegated that first year. Don't get me wrong, he was a lovely player, but it's amazing that the marketing at that time allowed that to happen. When you think about it, he beat Francis Lee, Colin Bell, Mike Summerbee, all these great players that the legacy of the club was built on, and it was all because of marketing.'

Perhaps Quinn should have tried to avail of that marketing for himself. The 6ft 4in forward could have used his aerial ability to fashion some kind of character that people needed to see. He could have modelled himself as 'The Premiership's Greatest Airman'. Okay, there's some work to do on that campaign, but there is something there, as he was known for what he did with his head.

Speaking of his aerial prowess, Quinn says, 'I was lucky that that was an important part of the game. Then Jack [Charlton] came along [as manager of the Republic of Ireland from 1986] who loved that kind of thing. I had great timing and that came from Gaelic football because I played in midfield there and you were going up for thirty, forty balls a game. I could tell when the ball was coming how I had to adjust and where I had to be to get it at its highest point, which is actually a skill in itself.

'In football, it's all well and good getting up and heading the ball or flicking it on but I had to learn how to pass the ball with my head. Tony Cascarino had what I would call a power header; he could bury it like someone would volley it. But I ended up becoming more of someone who would cushion the ball into the path of somebody. I started playing head tennis when I went to Man City. I wasn't very good at it [at first] but I became unbeatable at it. And I was unbeatable at Sunderland at it. But a lot of that was deft little headers. I remember one time when Arsenal were playing Sunderland and Arsène Wenger was asked about the game and he threw in a line saying "I'm looking forward to watching Niall Quinn, he's the best passer of the ball with his head that I've ever seen." At last somebody fucking noticed what I was doing!'

Quinn was much more than a creator of goals, he was a fine finisher in his own right – proved by the fifty-nine that he scored in the Premiership. Yet he is best remembered for his strike partnerships – particularly with Kevin Phillips at Sunderland and Robbie Keane with the Republic of Ireland.

In total, Quinn played in nine top-flight seasons – during which time the Premiership was rebranded as the Premier League – with a couple of spells in the Championship sandwiched in between. He was seen as a good player for Man City but morphed into a cult hero at Sunderland, especially in his final years when he got the best out of himself. 'My best years were my last five years. That shouldn't be the case, you should be fading away into the sunset.'

Perhaps there is a touch of regret that Quinn did not ply his trade beyond the Premier League in his later years. 'Looking back, I should have gone on the continent and travelled for a year or two. I turned down Sporting Lisbon with Carlos Queiroz and later on I was a whisker away from signing for a club in Thailand because I couldn't get a club at the time because I was coming back from a cruciate injury and nobody wanted to go near me. I would've signed for the club in Thailand had Peter Reid [then manager of Sunderland] not made a call. Now, I took a pay cut but I got three years on a contract and I repaid Peter by doing my other knee five weeks later.

'I was out for eight, nine months and I can remember cleaning out the stables, that my wife Gillian would have kept, listening to the Ireland games on the radio. The Ireland games weren't on TV at that time so I remember listening to Gabriel Egan and Eoin Hand call games and hoping that they would say that Jon Goodman or Mickey Evans weren't up to it and that they needed me back in the team. That's the way football is at times, especially when you're injured and trying to get back in.

'Years later, I remember being out in Iran with the Ireland team for the World Cup play-off [played on 15 November 2001]. I wasn't fit enough to play but to be there and see the team qualify was a fantastic experience. And then we went on to the World Cup in Japan and South Korea. That was all extra-time for me. It was my Indian summer and my most enjoyable time in football.'

On finishing his playing career, Quinn linked up with a consortium of Irish businessmen to take over Sunderland. The club were struggling financially and Chairman Bob Murray was ready to offload responsibility. Even though he had no experience in running a football club, Quinn took it on and began a different part of his life.

It was during those days that Quinn came to appreciate the power of TV and marketing. Some may suggest that is why he appointed former Ireland captain Roy Keane as the club's manager in 2006. If the Premier League was Hollywood, then Keane was a guaranteed box-office hit. In his first season in charge – and first as a manager – he led Sunderland back to the promised land of the Premier League in the type of way that was befitting of a movie script.

Quinn would move on again in October 2011, this time to the media. He had done some punditry and commentary through the years so he felt comfortable in that chair, opining on a league that he now viewed through different eyes. He still admired the football that was played, but he marvelled at the entertainment product that it had become.

From those early beginnings through to global domination, Quinn believes the Premier League has soared because of its embrace of television. The revolution clearly paid off.

2

Ray Houghton

Aston Villa (1992–95), Crystal Palace (1995)

Games Played: 105

Goals Scored: 8

Assists Created: 12

Clean Sheets: 25

Yellow Cards: 3

Red Cards: 0

Wins: 38

Draws: 32

Losses: 35

Talent is nothing unless it is celebrated. Or, in the case of baseball's greatest ever slugger, Babe Ruth, unless it is promoted. Arguably the most popular sports star of the 1920s and 1930s, his exploits swinging a bat redounded around the world, largely because of one man: Christy Walsh.

An Irish-American born in Missouri, Walsh was the first ever super-agent to grasp that sports was as marketable as any product that the Mad Men of Madison Avenue would push on consumers. He transformed the public image of Ruth at the peak of his career and therefore altered how middle-class America saw him, how the newspapers responded to him

– dubbing him 'The Sultan of Swat' – and led to the New York Yankees paying him so much more handsomely than before.

Ray Houghton could have done with the help of Walsh. Of course their careers never overlapped, as Walsh died in 1955, while Houghton debuted for West Ham United in 1979. Still, the sentiment stands that Houghton would have benefitted from having a shrewd agent acting on his behalf to finalise deals and sharpen his public persona.

It's strange to suggest that Houghton – the man who put the ball in the English net in the 1988 UEFA European Championships and who won five old First Division winners' medals with Liverpool – needed any help in convincing people of his talent. But he did. And he knows it now.

After the end of the 1991–92 English League season, Houghton had played over 150 games for Liverpool. He was a creative midfielder who scored important goals and brought out the best in his team-mates. He should have been Liverpool's poster boy for the newly created Premiership but instead he was transferred to Aston Villa that summer.

Forget about humble beginnings, the new top tier in English football was seemingly throwing cash around more recklessly than a gambler at Cheltenham on pay day. Surely Houghton should have profited from this? He was fresh from representing the Republic of Ireland at the 1990 FIFA World Cup and recognised by his peers as someone who had entered his peak years. Yet he needed someone to be broadcasting that to the managerial team in Liverpool to ensure that he was truly valued. Instead he was moved on.

Houghton recalls the period: 'My last season at Liverpool was one of my best; it was my best goals return, I was voted into the top six players of the year in the top division and I was in the running for being Liverpool's Player of the Year. So I didn't feel any reason to leave but it was just that Graeme Souness, who was the manager at the time, wouldn't pay me the money that I thought I was worth. So that is why I moved.'

The changes brought about by the formation of the Premier League were, for Houghton, clear to see. 'I think the big change was the money. If you looked at players in England [prior to the Premier League era], the likes of Liam Brady, Mark Hateley, Ray Wilkins, Glenn Hoddle, Trevor Steven, Chris Waddle, they all went abroad for the money. In Italy and France, where the boys went, they were offering more than what they could get in England.' Then that began to change. 'It didn't change overnight because when I went to Villa I probably would have got as much from Liverpool or thereabouts. And it wasn't as if Liverpool were going nuts paying-wise. I think it took two or three years and then it started, and you could really start seeing the difference.'

Another change noticed by Houghton had to do with agents. 'They were now heavily involved in football when before very few of them had a lot of say in things. But because of the change in the Premier League and the amount of money that Sky were pumping in, agents wanted to get more money for their clients.'

Born in Scotland, Houghton became a professional footballer in England, first with West Ham, then Oxford United, before joining Liverpool. But his Premier League highlights came in an Aston Villa jersey.

Leaving Anfield for Villa Park wasn't exactly a step down in standard at the time and Houghton didn't see it that way either. He embraced the new challenge and quickly established himself as a key player for a team with big ambitions.

'We actually finished second in my first season. We could've done with a little bit more help [with squad depth]. We brought in Dean Saunders after a few games and then we had Dalian Atkinson and Dwight Yorke, so it wasn't a bad forward line. Maybe we needed a bit more in midfield. There was myself, Garry Parker, Kevin Richardson, Tony Daley, Steve Froggatt. We had a couple of Irish lads in Big Paul [McGrath] and Stevie Staunton. Andy Townsend didn't arrive until the following season. It was a good move for me at the right time, in the sense that Villa played good football, Big Ron [Atkinson] was a good manager for me and it was the first season of the Premier League.'

Aside from swapping clubs, Houghton didn't feel any different in 1992 about football in England. Yes, the money started to flood in but it wasn't until the power of advertising was harnessed by Sky Sports that everyone started to see the Premier League in a different light.

'I must admit that I didn't think there was going to be much change other than the name of it. There wasn't anything to suggest that it was going to go to the levels that it has. Nothing changed with the pitches or the stadiums initially, so it did take some time. But then you had the razzmatazz of Sky. Putting on Monday night football, there was a different appeal to it. You could tell that they were trying to make it into something different than what it was before. That was one of the things that you had to get used to as a player, different days when the football was on … Monday nights, Sundays etcetera. It was a new product in town and they wanted to revamp it. Obviously Sky had paid big money for it, so they wanted to put it on when they wanted it … All of a sudden two or three years into it wages are going through the roof and players are becoming more well known because Sky are showing so many games.'

Whatever about how the game was seen off the pitch, what about the play on the pitch? Did that change much as the Premier League started to grow? Houghton thinks every era should be judged on its own merits and the circumstances of the period.

'I try not to look at what the 1980s were like compared to today because when I go to football grounds now the pitches are immaculate. You can't compare oranges with apples. It is what it is today; their training regime is completely different, how they are looked after is completely different, their meals are prepared every day by a chef, so it's not the same. The players now don't do long-distance running. We probably couldn't run at the speed they are running at, but they couldn't do the long-distance running that we done. You were running in the forest until you were sick during pre-season. They wouldn't be doing that, they wouldn't be playing on icy pitches. The pitches now are pristine. At Aston Villa they used to put sand on the pitch and paint it green to make it look like grass!

'Things did change with tactics and how teams lined up. The 4-3-3, for example, is something that I find difficult to watch with one striker up against three centre-halves. Which of the centre-halves goes to pick him up? How easy is it? And everyone is trying to make out that's it's bigger and better than it was before. There are teams like Liverpool and Manchester City who play football in the right way, but there are a lot of other teams who I find it hard to watch. The standard is not always great.'

Houghton has to watch it, though, because he is now in his second career as a media commentator/pundit. It is a job that suits him and one that he has excelled at due to his unrelenting love of the game.

For a man who has the unofficial freedom of every pub in Ireland, where a cold pint is on offer to thank him for Euro '88, Italia '90 and for chipping Italy goalkeeper Gianluca Pagliuca in the opening game of the 1994 FIFA World Cup, he prefers to look forward than wallow in past glories. He could go on about Villa's title challenge with Manchester United in the initial 1992–93 season, or winning the League Cup in 1994, but they are done now. They belong in the scrapbook, along with his brief stint with Crystal Palace that marked his last involvement in the Premier League.

Yet his view on how the league has evolved is interesting. Apart from increased wages and the influence of agents, what would be some of the noticeable differences that he sees in today's Premier League when compared to his own era?

'I think the size of the backroom staff at each club is greater than it ever has been. You go down to the pitch before a game and there are more staff members than players! In my time at Liverpool we didn't even have a physio, it was just Ronnie Moran and Roy Evans who would help you out if you had a problem. Now every club has its own full-time medical staff, including their own doctor, and even a psychologist so that the players have access to that if they need it. The players don't want for anything anymore and that's how it should be. There are also other things like a player liaison manager who will sort everything out for players. There is always someone on the end of a phone call, whether that is someone at the club or their agent. If the lightbulb needs changing the agent will get someone to come round and do it for them.

'I wouldn't know the extent of it, but certainly the amount of commercial stuff that the superstar players, like Cristiano Ronaldo, do is huge. I started to notice that coming in around about 2001. There was a lot more players doing that sort of thing. You wonder how much leeway they get to do that when it comes to training and the preparation for games. During my time you wouldn't have been allowed to do that. At Liverpool, it was a case of training then go home, put your feet up, don't go shopping, don't go golfing, don't do this, don't do that. It was literally train, rest and get ready for the next game. Whereas today footballers do an awful lot more.'

Footballers doing more or seen to be doing more? The work of Christy Walsh lives on.

3

Jeff Kenna

Southampton (1992–95), Blackburn Rovers (1995–99, 2001–02), Birmingham City (2002–04)

Games Played: 290

Goals Scored: 8

Assists Created: 20

Clean Sheets: 70

Yellow Cards: 15

Red Cards: 0

Wins: 97

Draws: 82

Losses: 111

Honours: Premier League

Walk in through the main doors, take a sharp left in the reception foyer, go up the four marble stairs that have been scarred with cracks that look like fault-lines in the aftermath of an earthquake, reach the start of a long corridor where the overhead light flickers, follow the grubby tiled floors that not even Mr Sheen could bring back to life and then stop at the last door on the left.

The door is old, its hinges carry the shade of rusted red, the window is cracked and has the scattered remains of a sticker in the bottom corner.

Inside is a classroom that can fit thirty students, with five desks each lined up in six rows. There is a larger desk and a single chair for the teacher, with a blackboard drilled to the wall and a wooden crucifix with the son of God placed above it – looking down on his disciples every day.

In the first row, closest to the wall on the east side of the room, there is a desk with a special marking. You won't spot it at first glance, so you need to move closer to identify the inscription and authenticate it. But there it is, in black ink, on the right side:

Jeff Kenna was here.

'Well, I certainly don't recall doing that,' claims Kenna when told about the marking. 'I wasn't that type that I was doing that sort of stuff so I'm going to blame it on somebody else.'

Perhaps the crime was committed by an old class-mate or some student years later who wanted to remind everyone that the guy playing every week in the Premier League once went to the school. Maybe it was an attempt to inspire someone into thinking that they too could follow a similar path. Or maybe it was just petty graffiti done out of boredom during one painstakingly long afternoon.

Still, it remained on that desk for many years as O'Connell School, off the North Circular Road in Dublin, took their time when it came to upgrading their facilities. The old Christian Brothers school is steeped in history. Named after its founder, Daniel O'Connell, it boasts many successful past pupils, but the ones who really make its students take notice are those who went on to play professional football. Kenna is its only Premier League winner, to date, but he was followed by John Thompson, Stephen Elliott and Troy Parrott in becoming Republic of Ireland internationals.

The fact that Kenna went to school there in the first place is odd. He was from Palmerstown, a suburb in west Dublin, so it required quite a trek each school day to get across the city via two bus journeys. The eldest of six kids, Kenna had two of his brothers – Thomas and Stuart – in tow as they were in the primary school across the school yard when he was attending the secondary school. That was the daily routine until he reached sixteen, completed his Inter-Cert and went off to join Southampton.

It wasn't a surprise when he eventually left Dublin for the south coast of England because he had been travelling back and forth on every school holiday since he was twelve years old. The club were determined not to let this talented Irish kid slip away after first spotting him in a summer tournament playing for Palmerstown Rangers. He signed a youth team contract, scrubbed the boots of senior player Chris Wilder, and did his best to impress as a midfielder.

Everything changed during a summer tournament in 1990 when he was with the senior team in Sweden and the regular right-back went off injured during a game. Kenna filled in. Little did he know that this would lead to his senior breakthrough with the Saints, who he became a Premier League player with in 1992.

Within three years, Kenna's star had risen so high that Blackburn Rovers felt that he was the missing piece in their title-chasing team. And when their manager, the great Kenny Dalglish, comes calling it is difficult to say no. A Liverpool legend as a player and manager, Dalglish had been brought in by the club's millionaire owner Jack Walker in October 1991 to initially return Rovers to the top division for the first time since 1966, and once that was achieved, break Manchester United's dominance by winning the Premier League. So there was no expense spared, especially when it came to the recruitment of players.

Kenna explains it all: 'What happened with the move to Blackburn was Alan Shearer and Tim Flowers had gone from Southampton to Blackburn. They were in the England squad when Ireland were playing them in a friendly in Lansdowne Road – the one that got abandoned. Well, that was my first time in the international squad. And that's when Shearer said to me: "I'll see you soon." I said "What are you talking about?" Him and Flowers were winding me up.

'In hindsight, I knew what was coming. The next thing was that it was in the papers that Blackburn were looking at me. Nothing official got said and then I was at home one afternoon when I got a phone call from Alan Ball, the [Southampton] manager, saying that I needed to come in, that they needed to speak to me. Straight away I'm thinking "Am I in trouble? What have I done?" They said that they wanted me to stay and offered me a new contract but they had agreed a fee with Blackburn Rovers and I had permission to speak to Kenny Dalglish. So I said that I would like to speak with him and see what he had to say. And it went from there.'

In truth, there was little real inner turmoil for Kenna in making the decision. 'Kenny is an absolute legend of the game. The fact is that they were up at the top of the league and they had been up there challenging for the two seasons. It was a no-brainer. I loved my time at Southampton and they will always have a place in my heart, but the reality is that we were constantly fighting against relegation. This was a chance to work at the other end of the table. And I also had international aspirations. It was a big project that they were building at Blackburn and I bought into it.'

The switch happened in March 1995 – in the days before transfer windows were put in place – and that meant that Kenna could only feature, at maximum, in nine league games. That was one short of league rules for earning a winner's medal. However, the club promised that he wouldn't miss out should they clinch the title – something they did achieve on the final day of the season at Anfield. They lost to Liverpool but that didn't matter as their closest rivals, Manchester United, dropped points against West Ham United.

'If you look back at that game we should have been out of sight. We had chance after chance but couldn't put them away. And I remember thinking: "Oh no, have we blown it?",' recalls Kenna. 'Thankfully it worked out in the end. We saw our bench jumping up and down because word had come through of the Man United result. For all of the work and the performances that the team put in all season, it came down to the final day and what a day. In the end, it felt like it was written in the stars for us.'

Decades later, Kenna can still remember the aftermath clearly. 'The Liverpool fans stayed and applauded us, so that was pretty cool. Obviously they were delighted that Man United hadn't won the league, so they were just as happy as we were. And at that time Liverpool were sponsored by Carlsberg so I remember them bringing in crate upon crate into the dressing room. It got sprayed everywhere, everyone was buzzing. We went straight from the ground to a place in Preston, still in our tracksuits. There we had a real proper celebration with people up on tables, lots of dancing and plenty of alcohol consumed. The celebrations went on for a couple of days; as you can imagine, the people of Blackburn were only too happy to allow us come drink in their pubs. We knew of the criticism, that people were saying that we bought the league through Jack Walker's money. And there is no denying that that had a significant influence on things, but the players still had to go out and earn it.'

The next few years did not deliver anything near the high of becoming a Premier League winner, but Kenna still went on to play in a lot of important games, including the following season's Champions League, and felt the pride of representing his country on twenty-seven occasions. Still, reaching the summit of the league – one which was quickly establishing itself as the best in the world – for a second time proved to be beyond him. In fact, he was part of the Blackburn team that suffered relegation from the Premier League in 1999. Injuries certainly didn't help his form during this time and he had to undergo two operations during a frustrating period that saw him swap Lancashire for the Midlands when he joined Birmingham City in 2002. That was a fresh chance of playing in the Premier League again with the newly promoted side, and it was one that Kenna enjoyed.

'Having just been promoted from the Championship [following a play-off win over Norwich City], we finished thirteenth in our first season which was a huge success. To come up and not be involved in the relegation scrap in your first year is a hell of an achievement,' says Kenna. 'We had a good group of players and Steve Bruce, who was the manager, was very good at getting the most out of players. He had a core of some very good leaders and I guess there was something that he liked about me because he trusted me to be one of those. We went on to finish tenth the next season but I left in March to join Derby. But they were good times at Birmingham. The fans enjoyed it too because we twice beat Aston Villa, their local rivals. I think even if we were relegated but we beat Villa the fans would've been happy. It's funny how football can be at times.'

A stint at Derby County was followed by a period at Kidderminster Harriers as he wound down his playing career and prepared to move into coaching. An opportunity came up at Galway United in 2008 as player/manager and he decided to give it a go. Kenna describes the experience as 'learning on the job', especially when he was exposed to the dire financial situation that had Galway's very existence on the line. Yet it was Kenna, as a rookie first-team manager, who the fans and club administrators turned to for solace. He provided it by keeping them in the Premier Division – by the luxury of a single point.

Surprisingly, St Patrick's Athletic came calling, sensing that Kenna might be more successful with a better support structure around him. For whatever reason, though, it didn't click for him in Inchicore. He resigned before his first season had finished. And that was him done with management.

Kenna now lives a quiet life, where the Premier League only comes into his thoughts when there is a game on TV. He rarely takes a visit to Memory Lane but you can see it in his eyes that some special moments still reside in his thoughts whenever someone mentions what he achieved.

Proof of which is hanging on the wall in his house: the Blackburn jersey that he wore on that title-clinching day against Liverpool, signed by all of his former team-mates. And below it, in the same frame, is the winner's medal that the club promised him.

The kid from O'Connell's did well.

4

Keith O'Halloran

Middlesbrough (1995–96)
Games Played: 3
Goals Scored: 0
Assists Created: 0
Clean Sheets: 0
Yellow Cards: 1
Red Cards: 0
Wins: 0
Draws: 0
Losses: 3

'The Brazilian boys were more clever than people thought they were. If we were on a night out, most of the players would be drinking pints of beer but the Brazilian boys would be in the corner sipping on glasses of Coke. Now, they could have had vodka or Malibu mixed in there for all we knew but the perception was that they were more cultured and professional.'

The influx of foreign talent to the Premier League coincided with a change of attitude towards healthy living among professional athletes in the early-to-mid 1990s. Keith O'Halloran was right in the thick of it as that transformation occurred at a time when the rebranded top tier in English football was starting to realise its global potential.

When O'Halloran first signed for Middlesbrough in 1994, the club were still playing at the outdated Ayresome Park and the squad was beefed up with rough-and-tumble professionals who were fond of their fish and chips before games and pints of beer after it. Within a year, though, that would all change as Chairman Steve Gibson paid for the creation of the Riverside Stadium – a modern arena that could host up to 34,742 spectators – and equipped player/manager Bryan Robson with a transfer kitty to attract new stars to the north-east of England.

Newly promoted to the Premier League, Middlesbrough were determined to keep up with the other fashionable clubs splashing cash on facilities and big-name players. The Brazilian pair of Juninho and Branco were the first to arrive, followed in the next season by fellow countryman Emerson, Italian duo Gianluca Festa and Fabrizio Ravanelli and Danish striker Mikkel Beck. Players of that calibre were not meant to sign for a club like Middlesbrough. Yet here they were on Teesside, ready to embrace the superstardom that the Premier League had brought with its packed stadiums, in-your-face marketing and bumper TV coverage through Sky Sports.

O'Halloran didn't feel out of place among it all, but he certainly knew his position. A boy from the sprawling, largely working-class Dublin suburb of Tallaght, all he ever wanted was to play football.

A start at the local Tallaght Town club led to a move to the distinguished Lourdes Celtic before eventually linking up with Cherry Orchard – a club with a reputation for getting players away to England for trials. Except O'Halloran was not one to rush any decision, so opted to avoid the traditional route, at least initially, of jumping at the opportunity to move to England. He wanted to finish his Leaving Certificate, so he would have some form of completed education behind him. He had heard the horror stories of talented lads lured across the Irish Sea with fame, fortune and football promised to them, only to return broken and broke. If he were to try his luck in England, it would be on his terms.

Equipped with the fuelling agents of aggression and determination, he was a player who you would notice very quickly in games as he won possession of the ball back before an opponent knew what to do with it. Broad shouldered and led by a chest that puffed out like the front grille on a 1957 Ford Thunderbird, O'Halloran was primarily a centre midfielder but also operated as sweeper for the Republic of Ireland Under-18s. Being able to scan everything in front of him allowed him to dictate play with his range of precise passing.

In many ways, O'Halloran was perfectly suited for the era of English football from the late 1980s, early 1990s. He had the right amount of what the Spanish called *furia* (rage) and compensated for his lack of speed with an ability to react more quickly than his opponents. His greatest asset, however, was his decision-making, and that applied to what he did off the pitch as much as on it.

One of the big decisions that he made upon graduating from school was to take up a scholarship with Boston College. Forget about England, he was headed to New England. Unfortunately, school was out for O'Halloran by the time orders were being made for Thanksgiving dinner. The sparse football schedule had him longing for something more regular. He returned home for a couple of months, trained with his old mates at Cherry Orchard and packed shelves in a local SPAR to earn a few quid each week.

That was his existence until Middlesbrough – tipped off by their Irish scout Paddy Fenlon, father of ex-Shelbourne manager Pat – came calling. They wanted to have a look at O'Halloran up close. Once they were satisfied with his fitness and ability, he was awarded a professional contract straight away. Not a youth contract, but a professional contract. The Dubliner would be bypassing their academy system to link in directly with the first-team squad.

A little bit older and more confident in himself, O'Halloran felt ready for the challenge of English football. He had to be, because it was an unforgiving world that he was entering into, a place where only the most resilient would thrive. 'You have to back yourself. It's dog eat dog. Without being over-confident and putting people off you, but you have to have that self-belief and that desire to get there,' says O'Halloran. 'I don't think I was the most talented player but I worked really hard at my game. I always felt that I had to work harder than a lot of other people and I think managers and coaches endeared to that ... somebody who is giving you everything because they know that they can trust you. I knew there were other players who had a lot more ability but they might not have had that desire and work-rate.'

That work ethic meant he quickly caught the eye of those in charge. 'I played in the reserve team. I would've played with John Hendrie and Clayton Blackmore. At the time, they were players who would give you everything. Bryan Robson would've played a lot of the games too as he was player/manager at the time. I was able to catch his eye by playing alongside him in midfield ... it was fantastic learning,' he admitted. 'The way it was back then, you were just a player. It didn't matter what age you were or whether you were coming to the end of your career or starting your career, if you earned the right then everyone looked after each other. Bryan let you know that if you made a mistake or gave the ball away but also if you found yourself in a bit of trouble he would be there to back you up. That was the great thing we had at the football club.'

O'Halloran arrived at a time when Middlesbrough were attempting to make the jump from the old First Division vessel to the shiny new Premiership cruise liner. It would later be rebranded as the Premier League, but everyone wanted to be onboard from the beginning.

In order to get there, Middlesbrough needed to clinch promotion and O'Halloran was determined to do what he could to help them achieve that. Not that his initial impact did much to convince others than he would be of great assistance.

'It was a bit of a nightmare, to be honest,' recalls O'Halloran with a wry smile when describing his senior debut. 'I played against Derby County in what was Division One at the time. I was asked to play right-back, it wasn't my position but you play wherever the manager asks you to on your debut. Derby latched on to it ... Marco Gabbiadini, who was normally a striker, ended up out my side. It didn't really work for us but it was fantastic to get out there to play.'

O'Halloran struggled to get back into the first team for the remainder of the season. 'The club was going for promotion and that went all the way down to the last game of the season, so I did find it difficult to get back into the team. But then pre-season came and [with it] a chance to impress going back into the Premier League.'

Middlesbrough had been part of that first season in 1992–93 where everything felt new and slightly unfamiliar. It had hurt the club, and its fans, when they became one of the first teams to be relegated from the new Premier League. This time, however, they were determined to learn from their mistakes. And this meant buying into the glitz of the new format, and bringing exciting talent to the newly opened Riverside Stadium for the start of the 1995–96 season. Certainly, since the Premier League's founding, the integration of foreign players en masse was something to which every club had to adapt. This was no longer just about football, after all, it was about entertainment. With the big stage in place, audiences demanded the biggest stars to perform each week.

'Juninho, Emerson, Branco, they all came in together [at the beginning of the 1995–96 season] and they sort of had their little clique to start with, but when they integrated they were unbelievable to work with and to learn from,' says O'Halloran. 'They had working-class backgrounds and playing football was something that they needed to do in order to provide for their families. They were living the dream of playing in the Premier League, getting more money than they would ever have been and having the profile to go along with it.'

Not that there weren't drawbacks to the move. 'They had to get used to living in the north-east of England too. With the wind that would come in from the coast, it was really cold in Middlesbrough – especially with the Riverside Stadium being on the dockside. You'd often see Juninho wearing a balaclava in training to cover up as much as he could.'

O'Halloran's Tallaght-teak skin could withstand the conditions better than his Brazilian colleague Juninho, who stood at 5ft 6in and had a skeleton frame that looked like it had been whittled down to make soup. On first impression, he wouldn't have filled anyone with confidence that he would make it unscathed out of a game in England's top flight. Then someone gave him the ball and all fears were allayed.

O'Halloran got to partner with the playmaker in Middlesbrough's midfield for two FA Cup ties during which he could easily have been yellow-carded for swallowing too many flies, such was the length of time that he had his mouth open in awe of his gifted team-mate. 'It was just a case of get the ball and give it to him. The things that he did with the ball were just outrageous. I was happy to let him do his thing because he was a genius,' gushes O'Halloran. 'Then at the time we had Nick Barmby ahead of him and Emerson was in midfield too. But one of the best players that I played with at that time was Alan Moore. There were times when Alan was untouchable; he was unbelievable … As good as Juninho and those players were, there were players around them who had to carry them and help them to have the freedom to do what they did. I think those players get forgotten about, players like the captain Nigel Pearson and Curtis Fleming, who, I hope doesn't mind me saying this, was someone who made the most out of his potential. He worked so hard and the fans loved him for it, and the players looked up to him because of it.'

As the season progressed, O'Halloran began to feel more settled. 'The more you trained and played with those players the more you felt comfortable. They treated you as part of the team. And there were times when you thought "I'm not that far off here." Most players are really, really good but there are those little things that make the difference – a bit of luck or they have that something extra. But when you're around them you feel part of it and feel okay at that level.'

O'Halloran was enjoying the fact that he was playing at this level, aware of just how far he had come. 'For me, I was given the opportunity to play and that is what I cherished. It didn't matter where I was playing or who it was against, I had that opportunity. I was a young boy from Tallaght with a dream to get there and had to go through so many obstacles and you constantly question yourself. Then you get to play with these great players and say that you've done it … it's a great memory.'

During his time at Middlesbrough, O'Halloran did notice how the flow of money into the game had started to change things. To begin with, Middlesbrough stopped training on an empty field at the back of a prison and upgraded to more suitable digs. And then the wages of players became a talking point within the dressing room, especially when it was felt that a high earner was failing to put the team before their own interests.

'There was a big culture change around then. The money was starting to come in and everything was kicking off. When [Fabrizio] Ravanelli [the Italian star striker, who just months earlier had scored for Juventus in the 1996 UEFA Champions League Final] came in, that was the start of the serious money. You could see they were getting forty or fifty grand [a week],' explains O'Halloran. 'At the time everyone is winning, we are staying in the Premier League and because you are winning games everyone's contract is going up as well. It would have been a win bonus culture. Once those players were pulling their weight and the team was winning then nobody had any complaints.'

When results nose-dived, however, the climate in the dressing room cooled. And the changes brought about by the arrival of some of the big names began to be questioned. 'When there was an influx of foreign players they largely integrated with the squad but when Ravanelli came in it was all about him. Everything had to be changed to suit him, like the food and how we trained. Everything had to be based around what Ravanelli wanted.

He got away with it initially but I don't think it was ever going to last as players were not going to tolerate it. A few times things spilled over and the players let him know.'

There was an inevitability to O'Halloran's time on Teesside coming to an end, or at least he thinks so. He wasn't, and isn't, bitter about how it ended. That's football.

'The reason why it stopped was because we had some very good players in the squad. You came in, got your chance, did okay but there were good players ahead of me like Graham Kavanagh, Phil Stamp, who had a little bit more than what I had,' he says. 'Bryan Robson was happy with me. He saw something in me and gave me my chance. But I got my chance because someone was injured and that's the way of it. Every transfer window the club brought more players in and you could see the squad getting stronger and better. When you have World Cup winners coming in, you realise it's going to be very difficult to play.'

O'Halloran only played three times in the Premier League and missed out on Middlesbrough's back-to-back runs to the League Cup Final in the following two seasons. A move north of Hadrian's Wall in 1997 saw him link up with St Johnstone, where he played some of his best football. Then another few years at Swindon Town followed before injuries got the better of him and a return home to Dublin saw him sign for Shamrock Rovers.

Having hit his thirties and fighting against his aching joints, O'Halloran stopped playing altogether in 2005. It was time for a second career to take his focus and that came in the form of becoming an electrician. It wasn't something that jolted his senses each day (unless, of course, he electrocuted himself) but it was a regular income.

That was until a route back into football came up with a multi-sports Development Officer role with Dún Laoghaire/Rathdown County Council. He used that as an opportunity to help start up a new club, DLR Waves, who entered the Women's National League in 2012 and are still going strong.

From there, he joined the Football Association of Ireland as a football development officer with a specific focus on women's football and teamed up with Dave Connell to serve as assistant coach with the Ireland Women's Under-19s. He won't admit it out loud but O'Halloran is living the perfect life: being involved with football every day.

The memorabilia collected from his playing days is safely stored in the attic of his mother's home. Not that he is ever tempted to open up that bag of memories; he would rather focus on what comes next. 'I never look back. I always look forward. I wouldn't be shouting about it, about having played in the Premier League,' he says. 'To get that far was amazing. Not many people get that opportunity to play in the Premier League. Even to play international football for the Under-21s. People might say "What about not playing for the seniors?", but quite simply I wasn't good enough to play for the seniors.'

O'Halloran is clearly content with his lot. 'I wouldn't be that person sitting on a bar stool saying I could've done this and I could've done that. No, I maximised what I got.'

5

Gareth Farrelly

Aston Villa (1995–97), Everton (1997–99), Bolton Wanderers (2001–04)

Games Played: 61

Goals Scored: 2

Assists Created: 0

Clean Sheets: 5

Yellow Cards: 6

Red Cards: 0

Wins: 13

Draws: 22

Losses: 26

It was on a drive from Oswestry to Birmingham that Gareth Farrelly happily embraced the news that a back injury would prevent him forging a career in the Premier League. Sitting in the passenger seat, he gazed out of the side window at the English countryside and began to wonder what a life away from football would actually look like. He was still a teenager, after all, so there was plenty of time to reinvent himself.

The driver, who was the Aston Villa physio, provided a soundtrack of sympathetic clichés in an attempt to soften the news that the Dubliner had just received from a specialist. Most young men would have been crushed by it, but Farrelly felt relief. He was relieved that the injury was real; that it was authenticated by a medical expert. And he was relieved that there was now a potential way out, away from the pressure of coaches who doubted him.

Farrelly had arrived at Villa as a promising midfielder who was meant to be fast-tracked into the first-team squad. It is why he was given a professional contract at seventeen rather than the standard youth team contract that most kids got. But a back injury put him out of action for his first full season.

Farrelly knew the pain was real, but nothing showed up on initial scans and club officials began to speculate about whether he was mentally fragile and simply not ready for the rigours of the professional game. He was, and he desperately wanted to prove himself, but the searing pain in his back wouldn't disappear.

He was afforded time to recover but when Brian Little replaced Ron Atkinson as manager the following summer time was up. Farrelly was expected to feature in the pre-season games and prove that he was worth keeping around. Initially it went well and he did enough in his performances to remind people of his talent. But then the back pains returned. That was when he was sent to see a specialist.

Farrelly knew what people were saying when he wasn't around or when he left a room. He knew that the macho culture of the Premier League in 1992 was unforgiving of players not prepared to fight through the pain in order to play each week. Injuries were not real unless they were visible.

The specialist, however, confirmed that it wasn't all in his head. He was experiencing growing pains, it turned out, as he had the 'lower body of a young man and the upper body of a grown man'. And even though the specialist suggested that his chances of playing top-level football did not look great, Farrelly was just pleased to know that he wasn't the weakest link in the Villa set-up.

As the Villa physio rattled off several possible alternative career options, Farrelly found his mind turning away from potential ways out. Instead, he began to focus on how he was going to prove everyone wrong. He would prove the specialist wrong. He would prove his youth team coaches wrong. He would prove the physio wrong. He would become a Premier League player because he was mentally strong.

***

Farrelly was always one of those kids who seemed a step ahead of everyone else. He was taking the bus from the Navan Road into Dublin city centre to attend Coláiste Mhuire before many of his friends had even figured out how to use a bus pass card. He was doing extra training – often going on runs with Mary McManus, a neighbour who happened to be a high-performance athlete – and seeking out new opportunities when his peers were waiting for it all to happen for them.

Maturity arrived quickly for Farrelly. Perhaps it was helped by his early morning trips into town, when he would walk down Moore Street, turn left onto Henry Street and stroll past the General Post Office (GPO) imagining what it must have been like in 1916 when boys not too much older than himself were part of the Irish rebellion that took over that building. He would think about the self-sacrifice, the desire to fight for something so big that it felt unattainable, and the sense of pride attached in giving everything to simply be Irish.

The sense of Irishness has always stayed with him. It was top of the agenda every day in his Irish-speaking school, where the teachers cared little if he represented the Republic of Ireland youth teams on the weekend in soccer as long as he was available for the school Gaelic football team on a Tuesday. He developed an appreciation for the Irish language, a respect for Irish history and a love of Irish culture. Yet he longed for a future that would take him away to England. The dream was to play in Lansdowne

Road with Ireland, not in Croke Park with Dublin. Either would have been nice, but soccer was his sport of choice and making it as a professional meant travelling across the Irish Sea to join one of the big clubs in England.

By that stage he had left local club Kinvara Boys to join Home Farm. He was attracting a lot of attention from club scouts, but his parents wanted to make sure that whenever he did eventually choose a destination it was the right one.

'I was very fortunate in that I had a lot of clubs interested in me. It was 1992 and the Premier League was just beginning. People seem to think that football didn't exist before the Premier League but it did. I could've signed for Man United but my parents were of the view at the time that Man United didn't give kids an opportunity. Aston Villa were the club that I thought I would be able to settle at and it was because of the youth development officer, primarily, a guy called Dave Richardson. People buy into people, no matter where you are. The scary part was that within three months of being at Villa he was headhunted to set up the youth programme in the Premier League. I believe my experience at Villa would have been a lot different had he been there all the way through.

'I got injured probably [within] six weeks of being there full-time and I was out for the best part of that season, so I found it incredibly challenging. I packed my bags to come home the first Christmas. I was of that opinion that if I can't play football then what's the point? I had been away from everything I had ever known back home and in Ireland you can be a big fish in a little pond so when you get dropped into this environment you don't have a real understanding of how football really works. You go from being coveted in terms of people wanting to sign you to being just a number. There are so many factors outside of football that determine whether you are going to be successful or not. Then that is determined by how you define success.'

Despite his growing pains, Farrelly did ultimately achieve success by becoming a Premier League player. There were eight appearances for Villa before he joined Everton in 1997, where he played twenty-six times in his first season. He also became a senior international when Mick McCarthy gave him a debut in 1996. The growing pains were gone and so too were some unhappy experiences at Villa where the old-style 'break them down to build them back up' coaching methods hadn't sat right with him.

So joining Everton was a new release for him. Everton fans will remember his goal against Coventry City in the final game of the 1997–98 season as he helped the club to avoid relegation. But his time on Merseyside was short-lived and he moved on to Bolton Wanderers, who ironically had just slipped down to the Championship because of Farrelly's goal. He would help Bolton get back to the top flight and rack up more Premier League games before clocking out at 61 in total.

Farrelly was a very good player; a central midfielder with a nice range of passing, an ability to get attacking moves going and a knack of winning the ball back quickly. Some may feel that he could have achieved more in the Premier League and accumulated more than six Ireland caps. He feels himself that he could have done more and a better grasp of the footballing industry could have aided him. Or, as Rod Stewart sang: 'I wish that I knew what I know now when I was younger.'

'In my case, and I'll be honest about this, youth is wasted on the young. You are absorbed with all of the distractions, the challenges around yourself. You live in a bubble in many ways and your world is very, very small. So I don't think you are going to have a global awareness of where you fit in or the value of labour or anything like that, you are simply focusing on being the best in your position in order to stay in your team.

'It's only later in life or in your career that you realise how things truly work. Then again you might never [realise it] because you don't really have to unless something happens that opens up a new way of looking at things. Sometimes you're not open to these things because you have not come across people who have experience of these things.

'Football, in many ways, is such a small part of your life [but] you have to dedicate everything to it. Equally there are other things you can do that can help you improve personally and open you up to understanding how the world works. For example, I'm a lawyer now, it's not something that I would have envisaged when I was playing football. I look back on my career as one of underachievement given the ability that I had. But that was part of my journey.'

After his Premier League days ended, Farrelly moved around to Wigan Athletic, Blackpool, Morecambe and Warrington Town with a spell in between back home in Ireland with Bohemians (where he served as player/manager) and Cork City. Then he moved away from football altogether to study law and start a second career as a solicitor.

Naturally his links with football drew him back in as he served on the Judicial Panel with the Football Association and the Premier League, while he is also a graduate of UEFA's Masters for International Players Programme. He also helped to set up a company called Player 4 Player, which aims to assist players in making the most of their careers during and after their playing days.

Nowadays, Farrelly is a busy man. His day job is as a senior associate with Bermans, a highly reputable law firm based in Liverpool, but he spends a lot of time advising players and fighting to alter an industry that should be doing more for its most important assets: the players.

The evolution of the Premier League, which Farrelly has witnessed at close quarters, having been there from the first season, has seen a shift of power towards players in many ways. The example of Manchester United striker Marcus Rashford, who used his status to spur political change with a campaign to provide school dinners to children during key periods, and released a best-selling book at the same time, is one that has sent tremors through the industry. 'Now there is an opportunity for people [i.e. players] to develop a brand which can actually surpass what their actual football contribution is and that is a massive challenge for the game now, but that is societal as well. Football can be extremely cut-throat. On a Saturday you're a footballer, on a Monday you're someone who used to do something once.

Depending on how much your identity is associated with football, it can be even more challenging to move on with your life. You may retire with a lot of money in the bank or you may retire with not a lot, but you will still face those same challenges.'

After spending an hour chatting with Farrelly about his career, his life and his views on the modern game, there is a feeling that there is still so much more to discuss. He is articulate, compassionate and easy to engage with. Perhaps the Premier League should hire him to visit each club to talk with players about seeing the bigger picture. Or maybe that is something that they do not want.

Either way, Farrelly will continue his quest to help players because that help is something that he wished he had when he first made it to the Premier League.

6

Alan Kelly

Sheffield United (1992–99), Blackburn Rovers (1999–2004)

Games Played: 66

Assists Created: 1

Clean Sheets: 18

Yellow Cards: 0

Red Cards: 0

Wins: 17

Draws: 21

Losses: 28

A spare room in Alan Kelly's house has been converted into an office with a corner set up as his own personal time capsule. On the walls are photos of his playing days with Sheffield United, Blackburn Rovers and the Republic of Ireland. On the shelves are books, trophies and other bits of memorabilia. It all serves as a reminder of Kelly's career.

Perhaps the most interesting part of 'Kelly's Corner' is the evolution of goalkeeping that can be seen from when he featured in the inaugural season of the Premier League in 1992 right through to the FIFA World Cup in Japan/South Korea in 2002. As you follow the timeline of images, the baggy jerseys move out of fashion and so do shots of him with the ball in hand as goalkeepers begin to use their feet a lot more.

Kelly is the perfect tour guide. His friendly demeanour immediately sets you at ease before his almost geekish knowledge of the Number 1 position enthrals you to the extent that you never knew goalkeeping could be so interesting. Kelly, you see, has it in his blood. His father, Alan Senior, was an Ireland international and a legendary figure at Preston North End, while his brother Gary played over 500 games collectively for Newcastle United, Bury and Oldham Athletic. All three of the Kelly Gang would go into coaching, unsurprisingly with goalkeepers. So conversing with Kelly on the subject of shot-stoppers is like asking a beekeeper about honey; you are going to get an impassioned response that will take up most of your lunch break. Kelly thinks about goalkeeping every day. Well, he is paid by Everton to do as much, but he would do it for free if he wasn't their goalkeeping coach.

He has helped design and deliver goalkeeping coaching courses for the Football Association of Ireland and served as goalkeeping coach for Ireland under Steve Staunton, Giovanni Trapattoni, Mick McCarthy and Stephen Kenny. If he were a guest on *Mastermind*, you'd expect him to nail his specialist topic.

When it comes to the evolution of goalkeeping during the first three decades of the Premier League, Kelly cites the introduction of the back-pass rule as being pivotal.

Laws of the Game: Law 12, Section 2 states: *An indirect free kick is awarded if a goalkeeper, inside their penalty area, touches the ball with their hands after it has been deliberately kicked to them by a team-mate, or thrown to them from a throw-in taken by a team-mate.*

Kelly explains: 'What used to happen was that you could roll a ball to a centre-half and he could kick it straight back into your hands and if someone wanted to time waste it was the most time-efficient way to do it. And you could do it multiple times to waste a lot of time. Also, at some of the European Championships, both teams would miraculously draw when they needed to get through [to the next round]. They would spend a lot of time kicking the ball between the goalkeeper and the centre-back. It was almost like piggy in the middle. It was actually comical at times because there was centre-backs trying to create space to chip it back into the goalkeeper's hands. Overall that rule change has been a success.'

Not that this was the only change over the three decades. 'Another big change has been the pitches. Now the pitches are beautiful, they are lush, but back in 1992 the pitches weren't great. Especially when you got to March/April time, it was more sand and dirt than grass. So there were probably more incidents of a bobbling ball and a lot of people will remember when a shot was hit towards Tim Flowers and it hit a marker in the middle of the goal and hopped over his shoulder. Those type of humps and bumps were a natural occurrence in 1992. It made it eventful at times without a doubt.'

While pitches are now expected to be as smooth as the cloth on a snooker table in the Crucible, the back-pass rule has had a profound influence on how teams play. A good example would be how a lot of teams have ditched playing two strikers who would press a goalkeeper whenever the ball was at their feet to a more modern set-up where the furthest player forward could be playing in a false 9 position, where they allow the goalkeeper more time in possession of the ball. This new way of playing has led to an increased focus on goalkeepers acting as the initial playmaker by passing out from inside their penalty area to enable their team-mates to build play through the phases. It was first used by Dutch side Ajax, where Edwin van der Sar would connect passes like a sweeper. In the Premier League, the likes of Fabian Barthez, Ederson, Allison and even Cork native Caoimhín Kelleher have become known for this skill.

It's not that goalkeepers didn't kick the ball before then, Kelly explains, it was just in a different way – mostly out of their hands or a rushed punt up the pitch. Sometimes the directive was incredibly specific. Kelly can remember in that first Premier League season when he was under strict orders from Sheffield United boss Dave Bassett to kick the ball to a specific spot. The intended target for the ball to drop into was around six metres in from the sideline at or near the halfway line, so the right-sided midfielder, positioned on the far side of that target, had enough space to let the ball bounce and then explode up along the sideline. No pressure, then!

As the Premier League continued to grow and attract more of a global audience, the goalkeepers changed with the times. There was always a steady core of British stoppers, but the arrival of one man shook everything up: Peter Schmeichel.

The giant Dane had just won the UEFA European Championships when he signed for Manchester United and his aggressive, animated approach was matched by incredible agility, clever positioning and superb handling. He was a star player just as much as any goalscorer or dynamic playmaker. 'In terms of Schmeichel, he changed the way in goalkeeping. You look at Manuel Neuer and people making the K Block and the Star Save. Schmeichel, at that time, was one of the main reasons why Man United won the title in '93. He brought an extra dimension to it. Not many would have been exposed to the type of goalkeeper he was, other than watching him in the European Championships. But now he was on our doorstep, performing week in, week out.'

Not that Schmeichel was the only star goalkeeper in the league. 'The mainstays of David Seaman and Tim Flowers were still absolutely top drawer. There were some exceptional goalkeepers in the Premier League and many who started around 1992 stayed on as they adapted to the back-pass rule and became even better. They changed as the game changed. But there's no doubt that some of the goalkeepers who came into the league brought a flamboyance, let's say, that made them superstars.'

Kelly didn't exactly reach superstardom himself, but he had his moments.

In the penultimate game of the 1992–93 season, Sheffield United needed to win away at Everton to avoid relegation. The pressure was on. Not that Kelly felt it as he nutmegged Peter Beardsley as the Everton forward chased him down. But Beardsley somehow spun on one knee to get back up and continue the pursuit. So Kelly repeated the trick and nutmegged him for a second time. As impressive as it was, Kelly could see in the corner of his eye that his manager, Dave Bassett, had run up the touchline to scream at him to launch the ball as far forward as possible. No appreciation for the beautiful game!

The other big change during that period was the addition of a goalkeeping coach to each team's backroom staff. Kelly had gone the first seven years of his career, at Preston North End, without the guidance of a specialised coach. He had to 'go figure it out' as his dad advised, right up until he made it to the Premier League. Ironically, his first proper goalkeeping coach was also a Kelly, but Mike was no relation.

'We used to look after ourselves at clubs. Me and Simon Treacy would do it five days a week and Mike Kelly would come in for a day or two – and we would hang on every word he said in those sessions. It was that first structured approach to the specific requirements of a goalkeeper. It blew us away. Suddenly from there, I think Packie [Bonner] became Ireland's first goalkeeping coach and it started to roll from there. I think around 1995, 1996 that is when specific goalkeeping coaches were brought in. Up to that point I relied on what my dad taught me, which was simplified down to four things: starting position, judging the flight and pace of the ball, making a good decision and being quick enough. Those four principles allowed me to go away and work it out. And that helped me, years later, as a goalkeeping coach because I had needed to work it out for seven years before I got specific coaching.'

In all, Kelly spent seven years at Sheffield United before joining Blackburn Rovers in 1999. It felt like going through a time portal as he left behind a largely British changing room for one that was almost like a United Nations convention. At one stage, there were thirteen different nationalities in the squad. That may be commonplace in today's game but in the early years of the Premier League it was quite a new thing.

Nowadays, Kelly coaches goalkeepers in a very different way compared to when he was the pupil. He asks a lot of questions, forcing the goalkeeper to problem-solve and think for themselves. In some ways it is an updated version of his father's methods and in others it is completely modernised. The use of sport science, video analysis and performance data means there is no arguing with the coach because the truth is there to see on an iPad. 'I can now get every angle, cover every blade of grass with a camera. When you look back to 1992 you still had the main camera. So that focus, the slow-mo, you get to see absolutely everything. Goalkeepers have to deal with that.'

The art of goalkeeping will continue to evolve and, as it does, expect Kelly to be at the heart of it. After all, there is still space on his wall for new memories to be added.

7

Alan Moore

Middlesbrough (1992–2001)
Games Played: 35
Goals Scored: 0
Yellow Cards: 4
Red Cards: 1
Wins: 6
Draws: 10
Losses: 19

Game intelligence has always set Alan Moore apart from his peers. For six seasons in the Premier League, it was exhibited through what he did on the pitch. Nowadays, it is what he is doing from the stands.

Responsible for the opposition analysis at Wigan Athletic, Moore is a resource that the club tap into so that they can outsmart and out-play the other team. In many ways he was their secret weapon in the 2021–22 season as the club won League One and promotion back to the Championship. Next on the agenda is a return to the Premier League.

Moore takes his job very seriously. He clocks up a lot of miles travelling to different grounds, monitoring different players and ensuring that he stays one step ahead of everyone else. That is pretty much how he played the game – always looking for that edge that would set his team apart from the rest.

It began with Rivermount Boys and was developed with Middlesbrough, where he fitted in among their squadron of elite players that arrived at the club in the early years of the Premier League. It didn't matter that his passport wasn't Italian, French or Brazilian, his technique and ability to read a game was on a par with many of his famed team-mates.

One of the reasons why Moore excelled was because of his honesty. He was honest enough with himself to recognise his limitations, but also to make the most of his skills. Add to that a work ethic that a coalminer would be proud of, plus a pair of feet that knew how to control a football, and you have someone capable of outwitting any opponent. And that honesty makes him such a fascinating person to listen to when assessing his own career.

Moore explains: 'My game changed over the years. I would have been a Number 10 or centre midfielder as a kid and then I ended up playing out on the wing for Middlesbrough because I was too small. I think I was a clever footballer. I had a good football brain as well as ability. I ended up playing centre forward for Ireland and centre forward for Middlesbrough. I played so many different positions because I could understand the game. I do think I had talent but my biggest trait was my football brain.'

Compared to when he started in the Premier League in its inaugural season, there is far more importance nowadays placed on game intelligence. It is no longer enough to be just a potent goalscorer or a battle-hardened defender; players need to be all-rounders who can adapt to different scenarios and execute a game-plan in the precise way that it was designed. The focus on technique and athleticism has not disappeared, of course, but it is generally accepted that the better players in the modern game are the ones who can problem-solve with the ball at their feet or react that second quicker than their opponent. It would be a mistake to think that these types of players are a new phenomenon, however; they always existed, it's just that every player is now expected to perform at the same level.

Moore describes it as 'taking on information'. That information can be transmitted to players in a variety of ways: a team meeting, positional meetings, individual meetings, on-pitch demonstrations, detailed training, video analysis sessions or access to data collection portals such as Stats Perform, Wyscout, Hudl or STATSports. It is a new way of learning and players must adapt accordingly. 'I've been an academy manager and I know that the only players that go on to the next level are the ones that take on the information,' states Moore.

'When I'm looking at players it will always be "Can he take on the information? Have they got a football brain?" There is that many talented people out there but a lot of them cannot take on the information at times and that's why they fall by the wayside and only get to a certain level.'

Moore has earned the right to preach to players about this specific topic because he has been there and done it himself. He thrived in a star-studded Middlesbrough team precisely because of how he used his brain. 'I know that certain players, like [Fabrizio] Ravanelli, used to like when I was on the pitch because I would generally look for him and he could time his runs then. Players do appreciate it. Football is done with a quick glance over a split second and that's how you know when to run and where to run. At those levels it's more a game of chess. When you get to that level, it's all about game intelligence. There are no words, it's all about movement, shape of the body, and that only comes when you are training with that level of player. We had world-class players coming into Middlesbrough, so everybody was upping their game in training, but that was set the first day that Bryan Robson came into the club. The standards that he set in training, without saying a word, there was no prisoners taken. Every day we had these challenges and every day we were getting challenged by new team-mates walking through the door.'

While Moore had the required skill and game understanding to keep up with the better players of his era, he also needed a toughness to compete in the Premier League, where physicality has always been one of its main components. He feels that that side of his game came from simply being Irish.

It helped too that Middlesbrough felt like a home away from home with so many Irish players on their books in the 1990s. While there were always two or three young lads arriving in on trial, the first-team squad was stacked with the likes of Chris Morris, Alan Kernaghan, Curtis Fleming, Keith O'Halloran, Graham Kavanagh, Keith O'Neill and Bernie Slaven. Moore jokes that they had enough Irishmen to field a full starting eleven and reveals that they all 'stuck together' – and that included when going out on a Saturday night! 'It was quite incredible the amount of Irish lads that we had at that time. You have to remember as well that we only had fourteen players on a match day in the squad and I think for a few of the games we have six Irish lads in that fourteen, which is quite something.

'We all pushed each other on too. There was a great togetherness there. Actually one of the things that I used to do was whenever we played against another Irish player, like Jeff Kenna or Denis Irwin, I would swap jerseys with them at the end of the game. I thought they would be keepsakes later on … It was always good to see the Irish lads because you assumed that they came the same way that you did because it's not always an easy ride in making it to that level. There was always a good camaraderie with the Irish lads and they always made a beeline for each other before and after games. The lads stuck together, except for when you are playing the game of course. I remember Roy Keane trying to snap me in two during one game and we had just been in the Ireland squad together a few weeks before. That's how it was, you went out to win games. And I think it was an Irish trait that they had that bit of steel in them; that's why they ended up going over [to England].'

Growing up in Dublin, Moore almost always had a ball at his feet. And that is why he ended up making it in England. He has a love of the beautiful game that is unbreakable and he has not lost the childhood enthusiasm that had him dreaming of lining out for Liverpool for so many years.

The closest that he came to that Liverpool fantasy was playing against them at Anfield. He got a kick out of that. He also got a kick out of beating their rivals, Manchester United, at Old Trafford. It shouldn't have mattered to him as a Middlesbrough player, but it felt good for the Liverpool fan that was still inside him.

Those days were special. Moore says: 'There were times when you were on the pitch and you look over your shoulder and see Dennis Bergkamp or Eric Cantona and think "I'm just a little lad from Finglas." But most of the time you were engaged in it and focused on not making a fool of yourself. It's good to look back and think that you played against all these great players.'

After leaving Middlesbrough in 2001, Moore spent a few years at Burnley before returning home to link up with Shelbourne in the League of Ireland. He may have been closer to the end of his career but his appetite for success had not yet been sated. Success can be measured in many different ways and for Shelbourne during that period, it was about progressing in Europe and dominating on the domestic scene.

Shelbourne had one of the best squads possibly ever assembled in league history when Moore arrived, yet he felt that he needed to raise the bar a little higher. 'I think the potential was there. When I came in I was still at an age where I could impact the team and I wasn't just seeing out my career. I did feel that my presence upped the tempo in training and upped the basics of passing drills and stuff like that. I had to take that on board very quickly because people were looking at me to set a standard,' says Moore. 'When I first came in, I could feel the eyes from the lads on me straight away. Obviously you're coming back from England ... but you take on that responsibility, you take on that ownership and you do set standards. But all of the players wanted to set their own standards too; the Owen Hearys, the Stuart Byrnes, they all had standards. We all lifted one another and that's why we ended up where we were, winning leagues. Obviously only for financial stuff we would have kicked on.'

Moore speaks glowingly of his former team-mates, including Owen Heary, Stuart Byrne and Ollie Cahill, who he believes could have forged successful careers in England. He even suggests that there 'wasn't much between them' when comparing Heary with former Sligo Rovers full-back Seamus Coleman – someone who went on to be a Premier League regular with Everton, and Republic of Ireland captain.

Three members of that Shels squad would go on to play for Ireland – Wes Hoolahan, Jason Byrne and Glen Crowe – but Moore reckons that the true quality that existed in that group of players suggested that they should have gone on to even higher levels.

Moore wound down his playing days at Derry City and Sligo Rovers before returning to England. He worked at a couple of clubs in various roles before landing at Wigan, where he is feeling re-energised and valued in a position that utilises his game intelligence.

Honest to the core, Moore admits that he has got 'plenty wrong, but also plenty right'. That is the nature of the job. Yet it is the consistency of his victories that has helped Wigan and could play a big part in their future, should they continue to listen to his views on the game.

To be in this position, where he is being appreciated, and paid, to use his footballing brain is the best thing he could have wished for – apart from still playing. As he says himself: 'I've not done a day's work since I left school because I'm doing what I love.'

8

Shay Given

Blackburn Rovers (1995–97), Newcastle United (1997–2008), Manchester City (2008–11),
Aston Villa (2011–15), Stoke City (2015–17)

Games Played: 451

Assists Created: 2

Clean Sheets: 113

Yellow Cards: 19

Red Cards: 0

Wins: 168

Draws: 127

Losses: 156

Honours: PFA Team of the Year (2)

During the course of a conversation about his Premier League career, Shay Given makes a bold statement by suggesting that, at one stage, he was among 'the top five goalkeepers in the world'.

It is strange to hear an Irishman share such confidence in their own status as it's not really in our DNA to stick our chests out and tell others of our qualities. Except Given wasn't attempting to do that. Instead he was matter-of-factly relaying where he fits in among the best goalkeepers of his era.

The interesting thing about Given's statement is that it should lead to a more broader question: how many Irish players can be considered Premier League greats?

In 2021, the Premier League created its own Hall of Fame and after two ballots only one Irish player, Roy Keane, had been inducted. Now, after thirty years, where does the Republic of Ireland rank among the 112 other nations to have been represented in the Premier League?

'Some great players from Ireland have played in the Premier League and we've definitely played our part, and it's nice to be one of them,' says Given. 'The next thing is to have some more coming through. I know there are a few lads pushing hard. During my time most lads in the Irish set-up were in the Premier League. We just need a few more to come through now.'

When he joined Blackburn Rovers in 1994, Given may have had ambitions to be successful but he didn't think that it would all happen so quickly. Given says: 'I was at Celtic as a kid and then I moved to Blackburn. The Premier League was on everyone's lips, the excitement of it all, the buzz of it all. My first year at Blackburn we won the Premier League and I thought this was easy. I didn't play that season, I was on the bench a few times. But that experience of being involved with the squad and training every day with Tim Flowers and Bobby Mimms was brilliant for me.'

Given remembers the sense of momentum that built as that title-winning season progressed. 'I think we got on a roll early on with [Alan] Shearer and [Chris] Sutton, the "SAS", up front and then [Stuart] Ripley and [Jason] Wilcox on the wings. We had a really good squad of players and it was a really tight-knit type of group. Everything snowballed right up until the final day against Liverpool [which they lost], but thankfully Man United drew with West Ham so we won the league.'

As the next season rolled on, Blackburn's players were considered Premier League royalty. Except for Given, who was still a squire waiting for his opportunity to prove his worth. And that came, unexpectedly, on 14 December 1996.

Before the morning papers had even arrived at hotel room doors, news filtered through that goalkeeper Tim Flowers was feeling sick and would not be fit enough to play that afternoon. Given would deputise for the England international as they took on Wimbledon in Selhurst Park.

Upon arrival at the old ground – yes, it even felt old back then – Given was excited. He had already experienced first-team football in loan spells with Swindon Town and Sunderland, as well as making his Republic of Ireland senior debut, but this was the Premier League. This was where he longed to be.

Wafting through the cracks around the door frame of the tiny dressing room came a concoction of Deep Heat muscle cream, fresh sweat and mud collected from the pre-match warm up. This was the aroma of match day and it ensnared Given.

After a thump on the dressing room door from the linesman (before they were upgraded to assistant referees), Given rose to his feet, took a deep breath and followed captain Tim Sherwood into a narrow corridor that funnelled towards a retractable canopy, which would not have looked out of place beside a battered caravan on a cheap holiday site. This was the route to the pitch. This was the way to his first Premier League start.

As they lined up in single file, the Blackburn players tried not to engage with their opponents, who stomped forward with gusto, as if they were making a dramatic entrance to a party. Wimbledon were known as 'The Crazy Gang' and they wanted the champions to know that their wild reputation was most definitely not an act.

'Oi, look at the kid they have in goals,' came the shout from one of the Wimbledon players as they all immediately looked at Given to size him up. 'Let's get at this keeper and show him what this league is all about.'

Given didn't take the bait. Sherwood swivelled his head round to reassure his team-mate by telling him not to worry. But the Wimbledon players were fired up and they were determined to rattle the young goalkeeper's nerves. As if they weren't rocking already.

Suited up in a garish red, grey and black jersey that was two sizes too big for him and gloves that looked more suited to a baseball pitcher, Given tried to compose himself as he took to the pitch. The home fans tried to unsettle him. They seemed to be just as crazy as their team on the pitch, especially since Joe Kinnear's side were on a run of eighteen games unbeaten. They were determined that this rookie keeper wouldn't spoil their afternoon. Except he almost did.

Given dealt with the high balls into his penalty area, the physical aerial battles and the scrappy attempts to claim loose balls that the *Match of the Day* commentator compared to a 'rugby scrum'. And he was fully alert when it came to making important saves.

'I knew that they were going to throw everything at me and they did. They played a lot of balls into the box and plenty of high challenges, but I had played GAA in Donegal so I was well up for it,' says Given, who pulled off superb stops to deny Neal Eardley and Marcus Gayle.

The resistance finally fell on eighty-five minutes when Eardley rose highest to win a header that sent the ball into the path of substitute Dean Holdsworth, who smashed in a half-volley from close range. The perfect debut, and clean sheet, had been taken away from Given.

There would be just one more appearance for Blackburn as he slipped back to being understudy to Flowers. That was until his old boss, Kenny Dalglish, took over at Newcastle United and offered him a fresh start. It would be a career-defining switch as Given went on to become a fan favourite on Tyneside and featured in the PFA Team of the Year on two occasions due to his stand-out performances.

The allure of playing for Newcastle, where the only thing that truly matters in the city is match day, is something that Given could not turn down. And even though the early years promised a lot and didn't deliver as much, he still enjoyed his time there.

'Newcastle are a big club and the fans are fanatical but I was there for twelve years so I just thought that was normal. It's a special place. The fans really worship the team,' says Given. 'The stadium is in the middle of the city and the fans call it their cathedral. They all walk from the bars, pubs and restaurants up to the stadium. It's a really special vibe on a match day.

'We had just finished second in the Premier League when I joined that summer. There was a little bit of a transitional period as Kenny [Dalglish] was going in after Kevin Keegan. Kenny wanted to put his own stamp on the team. Under Kevin the team was all about outscoring the opposition whereas Kenny wanted to get the balance right. I think that's probably why he didn't last that long [lasting only two games into the following season] because the Newcastle fans were demanding more front-footed football and a little bit more like Keegan's style.'

If it was chaotic for managers, even ones as lauded and successful as Dalglish, it wasn't any easier for players – especially foreign players arriving in the Premier League for the first time. The saying goes that football is a universal language, and it can be, but Given witnessed at first hand just why certain players struggled to adapt to the top tier of English football.

Some players, like Colombian forward Faustino Asprilla, were able to have an instant impact on the pitch, while others had trouble adapting to the weather, mastering a new language, integrating their families into the local community. 'It's not ideal if a player has limited English. Asprilla probably had the least amount of English but he probably let on that he didn't understand things at times. When you're doing team meetings, flip charts and video analysis, you don't have to speak any language because it is self-explanatory what you want from each player on the team,' states Given.

Sometimes, even trying to keep up with the tempo of the games could prove difficult for newcomers. 'I think the biggest thing for players coming into the Premier League is the pace and the power of it. In some of the foreign leagues, they may be a bit slower in the build-up and more tactical at times. In the Premier League it can be a bit helter-skelter. That's probably not the right word, but it can be ferocious and take players a while to get settled in. I think that is the case in a lot of leagues but certainly in the modern-day Premier League you have to hit the ground running. Players have to adapt and come through that.'

Other factors are also at play, of course. Given elaborates: 'Maybe sometimes if there is a big fee paid for a player and he's not playing so well the fans might not get it. But you have to understand that they may be coming from a different culture, speaking a different language, putting their family into a different city in a different part of the world. I think we've seen through the years that when a player settles into their environment then they play better on the pitch. You can imagine a player landing in Newcastle or Manchester having come from South America and they have to go to the local shop or the school for their kids, just how difficult that can be for them. I know there are people at clubs now who can help but it's still not easy to settle in.'

Given had to settle into a new environment too when he joined Manchester City in 2009. It was an opportunity to have a fresh start and also be part of an exciting new era for the club, which had just been bought by the Abu Dhabi United Group.

'It was a move that was too good to turn down. They had the money to buy any goalkeeper in the world and they wanted me, so that was a feather in my cap. I wanted to go there and show what I could do,' explains Given.

His spell at City had ups as well as downs. 'I played a lot of games in the first year and then the manager changes and things change. They wanted to get success pretty quick. [Roberto] Mancini didn't want me at the club anymore and he made it pretty clear that he wanted me to leave. That was frustrating, of course, because I wanted to be playing and not on the bench just picking up my wages. I wanted to play as much as possible. In the previous season I was playing well and felt that I was one of the top five goalkeepers in world football. Then the next season I wasn't good enough to play in a League Cup game against Oxford. So it was frustrating to say the least. When you're at a club like Man City you've got the League Cup, FA Cup, Premier League and European games, there are so many games and enough games to go around. But the manager wanted to get me out the door for whatever reason. You can try talk to the manager but it's just blah, blah, blah. The manager makes a decision and they stick with it.'

There was nothing that Given could do to win back his place at City, so he joined Aston Villa in 2011 and got back to enjoying his football. But his playing days were beginning to wind down and he accepted that, finishing off as back-up keeper to Jack Butland at Stoke City.

When he finally retired from playing in 2017, Given could reflect on a career that saw him playing for Ireland in a FIFA World Cup and a UEFA European Championship, collect an FA Cup winner's medal and clock up 451 Premier League games (a record for an Irish player). But, most of all, he can proudly say that he was one of the best goalkeepers of his generation.

9
Matt Holland

Ipswich Town (2000–02), Charlton Athletic (2003–07)
Games Played: 202
Goals Scored: 17
Assists Created: 12
Clean Sheets: 52
Yellow Cards: 2
Red Cards: 0
Wins: 65
Draws: 49
Losses: 88

Matt Holland spent a year as West Ham United's tea boy and he loved it. In fact, he believes it helped him become a Premier League captain. Well, maybe not so much the tea-making, but certainly the apprenticeship that he undertook brought him to the fringes of the first-team squad. It was there that he got a better insight to a dressing room culture than an *All or Nothing* camera crew could ever hope to capture.

Holland was born in Bury and spent time in Arsenal's academy before joining West Ham. He would later represent the Republic of Ireland forty-nine times – thanks to his Monaghan-born grandmother – and score a memorable goal in the 2002 FIFA World Cup. Oh, and he also captained both Ipswich Town and Charlton Athletic to their highest-ever positions in the Premier League.

Before all of that, however, Holland was a kid learning his trade in the unforgiving industry of professional football. He travelled with the West Ham first-team squad all around England, doing what he was told, listening to advice from older players and rushing to make rounds of tea and coffee on the team bus for whoever asked.

Then came the football, through loan spells, firstly in non-League with Farnborough United and then with Bournemouth. West Ham manager Harry Redknapp knew that Holland had potential as a midfielder, but he felt that some time spent in the school of hard knocks in the lower divisions should be part of his education. Holland explains: 'Harry Redknapp was a big advocate of sending players out on loan to get experience. A lot of it was to toughen you up and get ready for first-team football but also to realise how good you had it where you were in the Premier League.'

While at Bournemouth, Holland had to quickly adapt. The club didn't have their own training ground, the players had to bring their gear home to wash it themselves, they travelled to games on match days to cut down costs and their pre-match meal consisted of stopping at a garage with a budget of £2 to buy a packaged sandwich and a drink. Oddly, Holland sees the tea-making and loan spells as good memories – even though he never actually played for West Ham's first team. Holland developed an appreciation for earning everything that comes your way. It was an attitude that would serve him well throughout his career but it would never have been adopted unless he had gone through the hard graft of being a rookie player who did basic chores, which would be alien to modern-day academy players.

Holland believes that change has been for the worse. 'I think it takes away some of the hunger of the younger players. There is a hierarchy at football clubs and you are the bottom of it when you're a youth team player and you're coming through trying to push your way into the first team.

You are at the bottom of the ladder and your aim is to try and climb it. The hunger, I think, has dissipated a bit when they are paid as much as they are as early as they are and don't have to do the jobs that they used to do as well. I thought that was a great learning curve and a great character-building exercise. Now, there are probably too many players who feel that they've made it before they've actually made it. There are a lot of players who are on a lot of money but have not made a single appearance for the first team, so where is that hunger to get into the first team?'

Holland sees it as a major problem, though a solution is far from clear. 'I don't know how you solve it, don't know how you answer it because if you don't pay them X then someone else will pay them the money because there is potential in the young player. Maybe the answer is to pay him but hold it in an account until they are a certain age, maybe, so that they have that bit of desire you need to get to the top level.'

Holland feels strongly that the attitude of younger modern players does need to change. In what is a very male-dominated environment, how a player acts among their team-mates will often be dictated by what they see other, often more senior, players doing. That is what Holland feels can be the key to opening up a new level of respect and responsibility among younger players. He cites the example of West Ham captain Mark Noble, who was photographed sweeping the dressing room after a UEFA Europa League game, as something that sends out the right kind of message.

During his career, Holland, more often than not, was his team's captain. While he felt a little 'teacher-esque' at times preaching to younger players, it was something that he believed was important. 'I did feel responsibility. I always loved seeing [younger] players getting an opportunity and getting in the first team and almost taking them under my wing a little bit. I had Darren Bent and Darren Ambrose at Ipswich and Jonjo Shelvey at Charlton, who was only sixteen when he came through to the first team. Jonjo couldn't even drive so I picked him up quite often going to the training ground or taking him home after matches. You are trying to guide them in the right way.' Not that it always worked out. 'I remember Jonjo making his debut against Barnsley. He was only sixteen and I was thirty-four yet here he was screaming and shouting at me. I'm thinking, hang on a minute, I'm old enough to be your dad.' Despite what some would label disrespect, Holland could tell that, in this instance, the attitude was a positive. 'You could tell then that he had the desire and the right mentality.'

In the end, for Holland, it is all about having the right attitude. 'I always say that I wasn't the greatest player in the world but I certainly got the very best out of what I had. And I played at a high level because of that. I think that is why I was captain at a lot of clubs because managers recognised that and realised the attitude that I had.'

Holland's time in the Premier League had more ups than downs. The only major exception was when he suffered relegation with Ipswich in 2002. What made that even more confusing was that he was heading to the World Cup with Ireland that summer. From one extreme to the other.

He recalls: 'When things were going badly at club level it was always a nice release to go away with the Ireland team. Breaking it up and getting away from the club where there was a negative feeling, which there clearly was after being relegated. It was a strange one because you're thinking that when I go back I'm going back to play in the Championship instead of the Premier League, where we had been for the last couple of seasons. I wasn't too big to go and play in the Championship because my overriding feeling at that time was to help Ipswich get back into the Premier League. In the end, we didn't get promoted and I moved the following summer to Charlton, who were a very similar club in how they were run, and that brought me back to the Premier League. Ideally I would have done it with Ipswich as I had built up an affinity with that club, but it wasn't to be and you move on.'

Holland is remembered fondly by both Ipswich and Charlton. In fact, when doing some media work at the Championship game between the two clubs in 2021, he was applauded by both sets of fans.

There is more of a connection with Ipswich, he can admit, considering what he went through at the club and also that he only lives twenty miles away from Portman Road. He is a member of the club's Community Trust and is regularly invited to events. The Ipswich fans are quick to share their memories of the Premier League years and so too is Holland.

'It was enjoyable taking on the big boys,' says Holland of playing in the top flight of English football. He is also minded to pinpoint the difference between international football and that played in the Premier League, at least in the era in which he played. 'I think in international football you had a bit more time and space, the pace of the game wasn't quite as intense, but it was still such a high standard. Then in the Premier League you were getting that on a weekly basis by coming up against great players like [Roy] Keane, [Patrick] Vieira, [Steven] Gerrard, [Michael] Essien. That's why you play football.'

The boots have since been replaced with a microphone, as Holland is now a freelance media pundit/commentator. He goes where the work is but has a regular gig through Premier League Productions that keeps him connected with the league that he clearly still adores. It could have been very different, though, if he had accepted Iain Dowie's offer to take over Charlton's reserve team or if his application for the Ipswich job in 2012 had been successful (Mick McCarthy beat him to it). He had completed his UEFA B Licence with the intention of trying his luck in coaching, but an opportunity to work in the media simply came around first. Holland considered trying to balance both but advice from former Ireland captain Andy Townsend to focus on one proved to be pivotal. He has now been working in the media for thirteen years, so it's fair to suggest that his second career is going well.

'I go to games as a commentator and I'm watching it through the manager's eyes at times, trying to work out what I would do or how I would change it if my team was losing 2-0, all that sort of stuff. I'd probably be divorced if I was a manager because I'm the sort of person who lives it, breathes it, eats it and I would take it home with me. I would take defeats home with me and not be a nice person to live with. So, in many ways, it's probably the best decision I made, going into media rather than management.'

Typical of Holland's approach to anything that he does, there is always an element of self-improvement with regard to his media work. He will listen back to his own commentary and take notes of the best pundits in order to become that bit better with each gig. He accepts that he needs to do that in order to stay in the job, because, just like in football, someone is always scrapping to take your place. 'Sometimes I look at my diary and feel that it's a bit thin and I'd like to be doing a bit more. Sometimes I've got too much on that week. But as a freelancer you end up saying yes to things when an opportunity comes along. There are times you do worry about it, if your contract is coming to an end. It's a bit like football in that way because you are fighting for longevity and for your next contract.'

Despite the uncertainty, Holland enjoys his new role. 'Being still involved with football, and the Premier League, is something that I never take for granted. To be able to go to a Premier League match every weekend, to watch and commentate on it, is a privilege. I still get that buzz when going to a game. It doesn't matter which match it is, it doesn't matter where it is … the atmosphere, the buzz, the walk from the Tube station, the hot dogs, the scarves, the stalls on the side of the road, the teams coming out … I still love that match-day experience. And I'm fortunate to feel it in the biggest league in the world every weekend during the season.'

10

Stephen McPhail

Leeds United (1997–2004)

Games Played: 78

Goals: 3

Assists Created: 8

Clean Sheets: 8

Yellow Cards: 3

Red Cards: 0

Wins: 30

Draws: 20

Losses: 28

Only once in the entirety of his playing career did Stephen McPhail ask for an opponent's jersey after a game. It's not in his nature to seek out mementos or to even draw attention to himself. But this was different, this was Roy Keane.

It's not like he rushed up to the Manchester United and Republic of Ireland star at the first opportunity, like an over-excited fan at a rock concert. The Leeds United midfielder felt that he had to earn the right to engage with him. This was 1998 when Keane was arguably one of the best players in world football: a ferocious tackler, a master of controlling a game with subtle movements, a player who passed the ball with such precision that opponents felt like they weren't doing it right, a force of nature whose shadow loomed large when chasing down anyone who dared enter into his team's half of the pitch, and a leader who was able to inspire his team-mates and rally a crowd as if they were gladiators entering into the Colosseum with nothing but victory being the acceptable outcome.

On their first Premier League face-off in 1997, McPhail was just a fresh-faced eighteen-year-old. He wasn't sure what to expect from coming up against a player that he considered a hero when growing up in Rush, North Dublin and playing schoolboy football with Home Farm. Should he say something to break the ice? Maybe tell him how much he admired him? No, don't be silly. Maybe crack a joke? Don't you dare. What if Keane spoke first? What would he say? Maybe something like …'How ya boy, it's great to see another Irish kid in the Premier League. Can't promise to take it easy on ya, but sure we'll give it a rattle and have a few laughs afterwards. Sound good?' No chance. That wasn't going to happen.

Just compose yourself, McPhail thought, focus on your game and forget that you are coming up against an Irish legend. A gladiator doesn't become a successful warrior by asking nicely, they go out and prove themselves in combat. So that is exactly what McPhail did.

'I remember he clattered into me early on in the game. I clattered back into him and he just looked back at me, as if to say: "What you going to do next?",' says McPhail. The teenager decided that he would 'take the ball and make him think about what I was intending to do with it'. Would he pass it safely to a team-mate? Or drive forward with it? Keane didn't have to say anything, but his body language suggested that he respected, or at the very least approved of, how his opponent responded to the bit of pressure put on him.

It was a rite of passage that McPhail had to experience to prove that he could mix it with the big boys in the Premier League. Not that Keane particularly cared how a fellow countryman fared for the opposition – Ian Harte was also playing for Leeds that day and would have received similar treatment. Still, McPhail went toe to toe with Keane and came out of it feeling ten feet tall.

The pair would do it all again another two or three times before McPhail felt confident enough to make the request. It happened moments after the full-time whistle sounded to conclude a draw at Old Trafford on 25 April 1999. McPhail had run so much during the game that he felt a stone lighter and, as always when facing Keane, he had a couple of fresh bruises to signify that he had been in a battle. But the pair came together to shake hands and that is when the Dubliner muttered the suggestion of exchanging jerseys.

'We had played well in the game and as we shook hands I asked him for his jersey. He said "no problem" and walked away. I thought he forgot about it as we were on the bus all set to leave when the United kitman came on and said "Roy wanted to give you this" as he handed the jersey over,' says McPhail.

It was a token of respect and one that McPhail fully appreciated, even if within days of receiving the jersey, he then presented it to a Man United-obsessed friend of his from back home. So the only jersey that McPhail ever got from a rival player throughout his career now hangs on a wall in somebody else's house in Rush.

In many ways that is typical of the man. McPhail is someone who carefully sidestepped the glare of the spotlight, as much as he could, in the duration of a twenty-year professional career. He doesn't boast about his Premier League highs, his ten Ireland senior caps or playing in the UEFA Champions League. He doesn't have any souvenirs on show in his house. And he doesn't ever feel the urge to remind people of what he did on the pitch.

'Probably the older I got I thought that there is so much nonsense that comes with football. We're lucky to play an unbelievable game and you get well paid but, at the end of the day, it's a game of football,' states McPhail. 'You can get carried away with it, so you try to keep grounded and not speak about it too much with people. I like having a quiet life. Don't get me wrong, I love the game ... I wouldn't miss a game on the telly but when I'm with the kids or the family or in the environment I'm in I try to keep it as down to earth as possible.'

It could, or perhaps should, be argued that McPhail belongs to a select group of Irish players who never got to truly flourish in the way that their career path suggested they might when they were breaking through. McPhail was a classy player, a midfielder with a superb range of passing who zipped across the pitch without drawing much attention to himself. He was a technical player who had to adapt his game in order to become a Premier League regular. It was a similar story for the likes of Liam Miller, Darron Gibson and Keith Fahey – players who should have been afforded more licence to control the tempo of a game and utilise their playmaking abilities.

When McPhail first joined Leeds United, that technical ability was clear to see. It is why manager Howard Wilkinson sent word across the training pitches for the young Irish lad to swap the youth team for the first team. As he trotted across the pitches, with his stomach swirling like a washing machine on spin dry, he was stopped by youth coach Paul Hart, who grabbed him by the shoulders and said, 'Just remember when you go over that you are better than every one of them. You just play like you know how to and you will show them.'

Naturally a shy person who thinks before he speaks, McPhail was never going to make much noise when integrating with the senior players. He didn't have to because his football said it all. Not only could he control and pass the ball with efficiency, but he had the courage to want possession – even when under pressure. That is always the first indication of whether a young player is going to make it at the highest level.

McPhail had developed a toughness from his time in the youth team with Hart and Eddie Gray. He had also been able to settle into life in England very quickly thanks to the support of Harry and Ita Marwood, who ran the 'digs' that he and five other Leeds players stayed in.

Of course there were times when he felt homesick, but Leeds had a reputation for being a club that looked after their own, so he benefited from that. He also had Ireland international Gary Kelly looking out for him and the other Irish lads there at the time. Kelly, who was an established first-team regular and had played at the FIFA World Cup in 1994, went out of his way to help, even paying for flights home for his colleagues.

What helped most, however, was playing football. McPhail made his Premier League debut away to Leicester City in the old Filbert Street stadium in February 1998. George Graham had replaced Wilkinson in charge of the first team and felt that the Dubliner was ready to cope with the demands of a league where the football was played at a high intensity and juvenile mistakes were punished instantly.

McPhail adapted quickly and clocked up a lot of games. He was pleased with his impact, but one thing was missing – a goal. There was likely a heavy dose of relief mixed in with the euphoria when it finally arrived. 'The first one is obviously special because it was away at Chelsea. We went top of the league that night when we won. So that was one that sticks out,' says McPhail of his first Leeds goal. 'I was probably about twenty or twenty-five games into my career so I felt like scoring a goal was the next thing that I needed to do. By scoring it, it helped me get up to another level of confidence. It was a great feeling, amazing. You dream of those moments and then all of a sudden it's happening. It was a great time.'

Leeds were a relatively young team at that time with a lot of players having graduated from their academy, including McPhail and fellow Irishman Alan Maybury. A connection had already been developed between many of the players and, as a result, they played with a fearless approach, especially when involved in European competition. With David O'Leary now in charge, they established themselves as a top four Premier League side while marching to the semi-finals of the UEFA Cup in 2000 and to the same stage of the Champions League in the next season.

It was a glorious period for the club, and for McPhail. 'The European games were probably the icing on the cake for me. We got to the semi-final of the UEFA Cup, which is the Europa League now, and then a year or two after we got to the semi-final of the Champions League as well. They were special nights against great clubs,' recalls McPhail. 'We always used to have the hardest draw. But we had that togetherness. It was going from Saturday or Sunday to Tuesday and Wednesday games, just back to back. You didn't really have to time to think, which was great for a young player because you just rolled into the next massive game. That is something that really sticks out for me, playing Arsenal on a Saturday and then jumping on a flight to play against Real Madrid or Barcelona on a Tuesday.'

Hindsight has only made those European campaigns more surreal for McPhail. 'I only look back now and think that that was unbelievable. You see them now playing Champions League and I know how hard it is with the pressure on those games. You're not getting much sleep and you're back up to go somewhere else ... it's a difficult thing to do for the body and the mind. So when you see the top footballers now, it's incredible to see how they are playing.'

The good times at Leeds had to come to an end at some stage. With financial troubles mounting off the pitch, the Yorkshire outfit suffered on the pitch and were relegated from the Premier League in 2004. For McPhail, that was a chance to take on a new challenge. He says of that period: 'I played over a hundred times for Leeds. I'm blessed to have had that opportunity. But that day we got relegated I was always hopeful of being back in the Premier League within a year or two, but it didn't happen.'

He moved twenty-five miles south to Barnsley and played two seasons there before joining Cardiff City, where he would become something of a cult hero. 'I went down to the Championship, which is a completely different type of league but I loved my time there with the clubs that I was at. Absolutely I wanted to get back to the Premier League and I went close a couple of times in nearly getting promoted.'

The desire to help Cardiff become the first Welsh club to reach the Premier League kept McPhail motivated for seven years. Yet when the Bluebirds eventually landed in the top flight, his contract was up and he wanted to move on. The fairy-tale return to the best league in the world wasn't to be and he was fine with that. 'I enjoyed my time at the club and knew that my contract was up. I spoke to the manager early on and told him that I needed to move on, it was something that I needed for my own head. I gave my heart and soul to the club and loved it there,' he says. 'Helping the club get promoted was something that I wanted to do. I remember the open-top bus around the city, it's something that I'll never forget. Thousands of people out on the street and along the bay. It was a great way to go.'

His time at Cardiff was, in many ways, a maturing experience. 'I probably grew up in Cardiff in terms of personality. Obviously I was bit older, more mature. You obviously change as a footballer as well because you are maturing. I also had started a family then, so my off the pitch stuff was really comfortable. I think it helped that the Welsh people share a similar mindset with the Irish, as they are very honest people.'

Apart from becoming club captain and clocking up almost 200 games, McPhail's time in Cardiff is remembered just as much for the period when he was absent due to being diagnosed with Sjogren's syndrome (a type of cancer that affects the autoimmune system). The club's fans certainly did not abandon him. He explains: 'I got lucky in the care that I got and the fact that they found it early. Still now I get treated for it. I was one of the lucky ones. The club treated me so well and then the fans were outrageous. When I wasn't there, when I was in treatment, they were singing my name. That support ... you couldn't do without it, really. I'm forever grateful to the Cardiff fans. The amount of letters that I got from fans all over the country, it was incredible. I tried to keep it low-key. I played four or five games before I got my treatment – just me and the manager knew. I didn't want it to get out but I knew it had to [eventually] because I had to go into a cancer hospital for my treatment. When it did get out, I was probably a bit overwhelmed by the support. So I tried to get my head down and get through it. It definitely helped having that support, though. I remember turning on the telly to watch our matches and I could hear my name being sung. It made me want to get back onto the pitch as quick as possible.

Thank God I got a chance to do it quite quickly and it was amazing, it felt like my second debut. The support was unreal.'

McPhail would then spend one season at Sheffield Wednesday before moving home to join Shamrock Rovers in the League of Ireland. The legs felt heavy, the muscles ached that bit more, the joints creaked a little louder, but still his technique remained in those final years.

Nowadays he is part of the coaching set-up with the Rovers first team and helping to raise standards behind the scenes at the club. He is keen to impart what he learned in the Leeds academy and what he experienced in the Premier League, so that others can benefit. Just don't expect him to be shouting about it.

11

Thomas Butler

Sunderland (1999–2003)

Games Played: 19

Goals Scored: 0

Assists Created: 1

Clean Sheets: 2

Yellow Cards: 1

Red Cards: 0

Wins: 4

Draws: 6

Losses: 9

The routine was the same. Run home from school, push open the front door, throw the bag full of dog-eared books into a corner, grab a slice of buttered bread, change out of the school uniform quicker than Clark Kent in a phone booth, trample down the stairs, signal his departure with a shout-out to Mam and race onto the main street with the door slamming shut behind him.

This was what every day felt like to Thomas Butler when he was growing up in the Dublin suburb of Coolock. His life revolved around playing football on the street. School was just something that he had to do before the real work would begin on the gravel road with a battered leather ball at his feet. Kick-off would happen whether all of the players were in place or not. Butler knew how to entertain himself as long as he had a football. It was a bonus when friends accompanied him as they acted as team-mates or opponents, depending on whether they were playing 'Heads and Volleys', 'World Cup' or just a game. This was when he was happiest. This was when he pushed himself most.

They were simpler times when parents could trust that neighbours would share the responsibility of looking out for each other's kids as they took advantage of every moment of daylight playing on the street. If someone fell, they learned how to tough it out. Going home to cry about a cut knee would only take them away from precious time playing football. He would often return to it, longing for one more hour before his mam called him in for dinner or darkness fell and the lampposts' orange glow signalled that it was full-time. In today's football parlance, coaches and administrators would marvel at the amount of 'contact hours' that the kids were getting with the ball. But this was normal practice growing up in Dublin in the 1980s and 1990s.

There would always be one or two kids who possessed that little bit extra; Butler was one of them. Even after he swapped the Coolock streets for the Fairview Park pitches when lining out for Belvedere FC, and then went over to England to join Sunderland, that street – his practice ground – always remained special.

Whenever he did go back home – visiting as a professional footballer – the nostalgia made the hairs on the nape of his neck shoot up. Yet there was also a sadness to it each time. The friends that he once shared a brotherhood with had moved on, some to a dark side that none of them would've imagined as kids. And the absence of the current generation out on the street signalled, to him, that the kids are not alright, that they are not playing outside as much, that they are missing out on a carefree childhood.

Butler remembers the sense of independence that he was afforded by his parents. If he wanted to play for Belvedere then it was up to him to get the bus across to Fairview, to have the correct fare and know the schedule so that he was not late getting home. While he accepts that there are many reasons why a parent might not make a similar decision nowadays, Butler believes that something has been lost in that regard for kids – especially those with dreams of becoming a professional footballer.

'I feel sorry for kids now. I think it's much harder for them than it was for us. No social media. No phones. No hassle as the kids were always out on the streets playing football. I would come in from school, throw the schoolbag in the corner, then go out and play football. I had to be dragged into the house by my mam. Now it's a completely different culture. I think there is too much thrown in the face of kids. I teach in a school now and you're trying to tell them and explain to them the simple things and the principles are always the same: be on time, be coachable, show respect, work hard. They are the easiest things in the world to get right and I'm constantly having to reinforce it into lads.

'You'll see some lads who will see someone like Ronaldinho do loads of tricks and they'll try it. And you say to them, "That's Ronaldinho" or "That's Messi, you're you so just do the simple things." That's what people notice. I always say you're an Instagram player when [you're] just focusing on the tricks. But it's more important to be on time, eat right, work your socks off, go to bed early … if you don't have all these little bits around it then forget the other stuff.'

Butler has been there and done it; he knows how hard the road to professional football can be. 'Some parents are asking: "Tell me the truth, what's it like, how hard is it going to be?" So it's great for me to just tell the truth and say "Look, this is what to expect. It's not going to be easy. There are more hard times than good times." I always say to forget about the TV and Wayne Rooney driving a Ferrari because it looks great but they don't see the work that he's put in to get there. Generally the best players who I've seen do well have generally worked harder and sacrificed more than other people. This generation have been spoilt a bit more but that's not their fault in a way. You can't blame parents for wanting the best for their kids.'

The path to professional football for aspiring young players has more pitfalls and obstacles than a journey from the Shire to Mordor. Yet it is a route that thousands of kids begin to take long before stubble has aged their baby face.

Butler admits that he was too young when he left Dublin for Sunderland as a sixteen-year-old. He had offers from various clubs, given that he was a classy midfielder who could glide across the pitch and act as a creative fulcrum for his team. Advice from his older brother, John, ultimately swayed him to take a chance on joining a team in the English Championship.

'My brother was at Leeds, who had a fantastic youth team at the time, and I told him that Sunderland had offered me a trial. I was a young lad and I was thinking that I'd like to play for a team in the Premier League. But my brother said, "Go play for Sunderland because they are an up-and-coming team and you've got more of a chance there." He was aware of his situation at Leeds, where he was fourth, fifth or sixth choice for right-back, so he knew that I had more of a chance at somewhere like Sunderland who didn't have as many players. So it was on his advice that I went to Sunderland and it turned out to be the right decision.'

Butler broke into the first-team set-up in 1999 and played nineteen times in the Premier League over three seasons. He should've played a lot more, only for a litany of injuries that disrupted any sort of rhythm he tried to build. He should've been a Formula One car, but he ended up like Chitty Chitty Bang Bang – only able to produce moments of magic when consistency was what he desired most. Still, he is grateful for the experience.

'It's the best feeling in the world,' says Butler of playing in the Premier League. 'We played Man United at home ... Roy Keane, David Beckham and I'm lining up alongside them in the tunnel, a young lad from Coolock. They are memories that you'll always have. You get a bit of stick, even now, with people saying: "You only played nineteen games". But if someone had told me that I would only play one game in the Premier League, I would go back and relive it all again. I knew that I could play in the Premier League. I was Man of the Match a couple of times. I played at Highbury, I've come on at half-time against [Dennis] Bergkamp and [Thierry] Henry and all these, and I've basically been told that I was the best player on the pitch. I didn't feel out of place.'

Yet he walked away from it all. Still under contract at Sunderland, he asked to rip up his contract. He had had enough. Four hamstring tears in one season, training feeling like 'schoolwork' and a difficulty in dealing with the loneliness of being away from the squad when injured had brought him to his decision. The experience of professional football had gone stale.

In hindsight, perhaps Butler should have requested a transfer to another club and made a fresh start. But he returned to Dublin to get away from it all. There was no real explanation given so some of the tabloid newspapers stirred up the speculation by suggesting that he had gone AWOL.

He simply needed a break. And that is what he got for three or four months. He returned to the house he grew up in, to the street where his love of football was fostered. There was never a feeling that he was done with the game, it was just that he was done with Sunderland after six years.

It didn't take long before he got going again. A move to Scotland to join Dunfermline Athletic got his engine fired up and that led to a move to Hartlepool United in 2005. He was back playing regularly – even if the injuries never fully disappeared – and people started to take notice. Just a year later, he dropped down to League One to sign for Swansea City as he felt that the club was on the cusp of doing big things. Except he almost didn't get the green light for it to happen.

'I remember going to Swansea for my medical and the physio is going, "I can't believe we are signing this player." He was going through the list of operations from my injuries and he must have had about twenty pages: 1998 hamstring tear, 1998 calf tear, 2000 rupture, hernia, operation on ankle, operation on other ankle, operation on this, operation on that. It's like having a car that has been in seven car crashes. Sometimes you're a bit critical of yourself – ah, I should've done better there and there. But I'm at the age now where I'm proud that I got that far, especially considering that I sustained so much trauma to my body.'

Butler stayed with Swansea as they achieved a couple of promotions to eventually reach the Premier League. However, he didn't get to complete that fairy-tale return to the pitch in England's top division as the injuries had caught up with him. Still, he gave it everything and there is no shame in that.

Some players struggle to accept the end of their playing career at a certain level, Butler jokes that he's glad to have entered into his forties because the pace of the Over-40s League is now perfectly suited to his battered body as he plays with friends simply for the enjoyment of it.

He still lives in the Sunderland area and looks out for their results. He is proud of his career, which included two Republic of Ireland senior caps, and of what he did in those nineteen Premier League games. If he was bitter about the game for a period of his life, he is now grateful to still be part of it, even if that is by coaching kids in St Joseph's, Headbourne.

It is Butler's job to prepare the kids for a potential life as a professional footballer. He can immediately spot the ones who have the hunger for it but even they need to learn that it takes a hell of a lot to make it all the way. That is something he is passionate about; sending out the right messages and being honest about the journey.

He wishes the Premier League would do the same, by preparing young players for the knock-backs, as most will experience failure in the pursuit of a full-time contract. 'I think they don't show enough [of that reality of the game]. You don't want to put players off but I think they should be honest and have documentaries on and bring players in who haven't made it. Have someone who kids all say "he's going to be a player" and interview him and let him say what he had to go through. Show them suffering in a way, show them coming back from a six-month operation and show them the rehab and then the breakdown again.

'When I was at Sunderland, we had sixteen players in our youth team and I think two lads got offered pro contracts. So you can imagine the lads going in to be told that they are not good enough. I was sitting there seeing it, the lads coming out bawling their eyes out. They're your mates who you've lived with and trained with every day for two years. All they wanted to do was play football, now they don't know what to do. But that sort of stuff is not shown.

'If they showed that kind of stuff I think people would be more sympathetic. People automatically assume, "Ah, you're a footballer, you're a millionaire, you're this, that and the other." But that's only a tiny per cent. The vast majority of lads who play in League Two earn £50,000 a year, they'll have a missus, kids, bills, cars. People will think that £50,000 a year is loads and it is a good wage but the mentality is that "Oh, you play for Carlisle, you must be on £10,000 a week." No chance. Yes, the top players in the Premier League live like movie stars, but they've had to work ridiculously hard on top of being unbelievably talented and having a bit of luck. That is what needs to be shown.'

Butler has been there and battled through it. He knows about the ecstatic highs and the crushing lows. He can attest to just why the Premier League is a special league. He can talk about how hard work does pay off. And whenever he returns to the street outside his family home in Coolock, he can crack a smile, knowing that he made it. He lived his dream.

12

Rory Delap

Derby County (1997–2001), Southampton (2001–05),
Sunderland (2005–06), Stoke City (2008–12)

Games Played: 359

Goals Scored: 23

Assists Created: 21

Clean Sheets: 80

Yellow Cards: 46

Red Cards: 4

Wins: 106

Draws: 103

Losses: 150

The first time it happened, it raised eyebrows and led to a flurry of questions. It was a very innocent request but one that showcased a changing of culture, or, depending on one's interpretation, a betrayal of roots. All Rory Delap did was ask for some olive oil! Except this wasn't the type of ordinary condiment that belonged on an English table. This was an Italian import that signalled that foreign influences were beginning to infiltrate Her Majesty's realm.

Delap had been watching Stefano Eranio. The former AC Milan winger had arrived at Derby County in 1997 and brought with him a 'continental' way of doing things. It was all new and so foreign. Delap paints the picture: 'I remember looking at Eranio and everything that he did ... the food that he ate, putting olive oil on everything, how he would stretch every day before and after training. I remember seeing him put salt on his bread and him saying that he doesn't drink orange juice because it dehydrates you. I used to think that eating loads of pasta was good for you but he only ate a small portion – more of a starter, really. Everything he did was so professional.'

Forget about foreign players adapting to a British diet, they arrived into the Premier League with their own way of doing things and it was up to others to adapt to their quirks. Delap paid attention, trying to identify Eranio's secret to being so agile while in his thirties. Perhaps it was in the olive oil.

Developing good habits allowed Delap attain his own longevity when it came to his playing career. In total, he featured in fourteen different Premier League seasons and sits seventh on the list of Irish players with the most appearances in that division. Not bad for a kid who started out at Carlisle United.

Born in England's West Midlands, Delap qualified for the Republic of Ireland through a father from Donegal and a mother from Meath. He is fiercely proud of his Irish roots and, arguably, should have collected more than eleven senior caps. Certainly his consistency in the Premier League with Derby, Southampton, Sunderland and Stoke City suggests that he should have featured more.

Similar to an animal adapting to new habitats, Delap continually found a way to be whatever a manager needed him to be. Whether that was in midfield, on the wing or even at full-back, he excelled. Not that it always came easy to him. Maybe his introduction to Premier League football had toughened him up at just the right time. 'My first two appearances were Everton away and then Man United away. At that time Man United were probably the best team in Europe. I gave away a penalty in the game – to

Denis Irwin, actually. I got a bollocking afterwards and I was left out for the next game. You learn quickly.'

Learning the game was relatively easy in those days at Derby because manager Jim Smith created an environment that encouraged everyone to contribute. He signed players as much for their character as their footballing technique and he was always searching for an edge. It's why the club were among the first to use Prozone technology, which monitored players' performances and translated it into data.

Delap struggled at first to compute the different sets of statistics. 'You were given all of these things, like how many times I passed the ball to someone, or someone passed the ball to me, or when I tended to fade in games. My head was spinning when I was going through it. But it was all part of that relationship from the physio to the S and C [strength and conditioning] coach to the assistant coach to the manager. Everyone was trying to understand it because everyone had to be on the same page, otherwise it could be detrimental to the team if not used correctly.'

Having tip-toed his way through the initial minefield of performance analysis, Delap came to understand its importance. 'Whether you are playing the old Wimbledon-style football or the tiki-taka style of Barcelona, you have to understand why the full-back receives more of the ball than the centre-back or midfielder, or why the full-back plays the ball to his winger and not into his midfielder. All of those things come into it.'

Of course, statistics can be manipulated too. For example, a player may boast about their running distance or high-intensity sprints, but they may not have used the ball well during a game. It is how the data is understood by the players that matters most. That is something that Delap made the most of and believes that younger players need to master. If they don't understand something then he feels that they must gain the courage to say so. It is the players who stay quiet and don't take the information on who slip away, no matter how talented they may be.

On the other hand, sometimes a player can take it too far. Delap laughs when remembering how a player wanted a second assist bonus inserted into their contract. He sees the absurdity of claiming direct influence on a goal when they may have only played an initial ten-yard pass but others did the hard work, how it is almost like a pawn taking credit for the queen's checkmate move in a game of chess.

If bonuses had been given out for special contributions, then Delap would have made a small fortune off the back of his trademark long throw-in. It was such an effective weapon that many teams feared seeing the ball go out of play in their defensive third because they knew what was coming next. A ball kid would be on standby with a towel to wipe the ball down and present it to Delap, who would then catapult it over the first line of defence in the hope that a team-mate could then direct it into the back of the net.

It almost feels like an insult to mention the throw-in to Delap. He should be spending time talking about his ability as a ball-winning midfielder who had an engine that never seemed to overheat or burn out. He created goalscoring opportunities, he finished off goalscoring opportunities (twenty-three times in the Premier League) and he generally made his teams that bit better. Yet it is the long throw-in that people want to quiz him on most. 'I get asked a lot about it and, to be honest, I'm not too bothered about it. I think the first interview I did about it I had played nearly 250 Premier League games, so it wasn't the be-all and end-all.'

It was during his time at Stoke that the long throw-in became something of his signature move. 'I think it was more about the time and the club I was at. It just ballooned really, it was crazy seeing the reaction to it. It's weird because I've had people at Carlisle, Derby, Southampton and Sunderland ask me where was it when I played for them. But I did use it all the way through my career to various degrees, but when I was at Stoke I was six foot and one of the smallest. It was the land of the giants. So that was more to do with it than anything else. Tony Pulis [former Stoke City manager] said that it was something that we could utilise and that was even before I had met him. He's not daft, he knows every player that he works with so he knew that I had that attribute.'

Not that everyone liked to see it. Certainly opposition fans did their best to distract him. 'I got battered. I hated going to the smaller grounds because the sideline was that bit closer to the fans. I would be getting slaps, spat on, everything. It wasn't as glamorous as people might think it was.'

Delap knows all about the different sides of the Premier League and he remains vigilant on how young players work their way through the academy systems. He has seen it first-hand as a player, as a coach and as a parent. His eldest son, Liam, is on the books at Manchester City and has already played in the Premier League while still a teenager. He is a different type of player from his father, mainly playing as a striker. And he has opted to represent England at international level. Those are the types of decision that Delap has entrusted his son to make on his own.

It is similar with his younger son, Finn, who is attempting to forge a career at Burton Albion. Delap wants the best for his boys and hopes that they succeed in becoming professional footballers, but they have to achieve it on their own terms. 'You often see it with younger players that the parents want it more than the player. I've seen it all the way through in various different roles; one as a parent on the sidelines, two as a coach – I worked with the Under-13s up to Under-21s at Derby. Some of the pressure put on kids by their parents is horrific, sometimes they are under pressure to almost provide for their family. I leave Liam to himself. If he ever asks for my advice I will give it; he might take it or he might not. It's the same with my other lad, Finn. He was released by Derby and went down the trial route but has landed at Burton Albion. Sometimes they ask my advice, sometimes they don't. I'd like to think that we've brought them up to make good decisions.'

One thing that the two lads do engage with their father on is 'taking the piss' whenever they come across clips of his playing days. That long throw-in is far from praised within the Delap household when the boys are bringing their old man back down to earth.

13

Richard Dunne

Everton (1996–2000), Manchester City (2000–01, 2002–09),
Aston Villa (2009–12), Queens Park Rangers (2014–15)
Games Played: 431
Goals: 11
Assists Created: 5
Clean Sheets: 107
Yellow Cards: 74
Red Cards: 8
Wins: 136
Draws: 120
Losses: 175
Honours: PFA Team of the Year

Richard Dunne is a fascinating person to listen to on the topic of the Premier League. Just don't ask him about his own experiences. Whether he is a voice for hire on TV or just shooting the breeze with a random football fan, he is opinionated, honest and able to provide an insightful analysis of a game or incident in a concise way.

A giant figure whose shadow will ensnare you before you even hear his footsteps coming, Dunne was part of the last bastion of centre-backs who were known for aerial duels more than building play from the back. The Dubliner knew how to pass the ball, of course, it was just a different era that he played in.

In thirty years of the Premier League, Dunne would be considered by many to be among the very best defenders. The stats certainly back that up, as he was a regular with four different clubs and scored eleven goals (eight of which were headers). So it's tempting to ask him – do any of the goals stand out?

'Not really, no,' says Dunne in a deadpan type of way. 'To be fair, I don't really look back on what happened. It's something that I did and now I'm on to the next period of my life. I've been asked to do certain things where you look back over your career and I've no real massive interest in it. If anyone wants to find anything out it's all there. I've done interviews and spoke about stuff a million times [during his career], but now that I'm coaching kids I'm more looking forward. I'm more looking at football now, seeing what people are doing and what is the next aspect.'

He has no real interest in exploring the past. He hammers the point home as firmly as one of those eight headed goals. 'I used to play football and that sort of stuff. It happened. I don't want it to be all that I am. I've got other stuff that I'm interested in and that's what occupies my time rather than telling everybody that I used to be a footballer. There are loads of people who like doing that and there are loads of people who don't like it. You finish football at thirty-five or whatever, so you have to decide if you want to go on the circuit of being the ex-footballer or if you want to move forward and do something different. For me, I did my football career and I loved it. I'm very proud that I played in the Premier League and very proud that I played for Ireland, but it's not something that I need to keep going over all of the time.'

Dunne's journey to the Premier League almost didn't happen. Even though he was excelling as a schoolboy player with Home Farm – who had links with Everton at the time – he wasn't being pushed forward for a trial with the Toffees because of nepotism. Or at least a fear on the part of his Uncle Theo, who was a coach at Home Farm, that people would see it that way. 'He [Theo] wouldn't send me over. He sent a couple of lads from my Home Farm team over for trials but never really pushed me to go because of the family connection and didn't want to be seen to be doing favours. So I ended up going on trial with Nottingham Forest,' shares Dunne. 'I went over to Forest and played a youth team game, I think it was against Man United. I had a really nice time there, they took us to the FA Cup Final later on in the year. There were a few of us going over there at the time, I think myself, Stephen McPhail, David Freeman and a couple of others. But then I ended up going to Everton and that was that.'

Everything worked out in the end. There was no falling out with his uncle and his father, Dick, was delighted because he was an Everton fan. It was now up to Dunne to show that he could forge a career at the club.

It helped that Dunne was as tough as a rhino's hide because the first box to tick on the entrance exam to the 'Centre-Back Club' was: 'Are you strong enough?' Forget about fancy football, this was an era when bloody noses and bandaged foreheads were in fashion. And that suited the streetwise kid from Tallaght just fine.

Word spread around the club of Dunne's development. He may have been in the academy system but he was playing like a man, standing up to each challenge while others became hide-and-seek captains when the going got rough. So it made perfect sense when he was promoted to the first-team squad in 1996.

In the dressing room were FA Cup winners and seasoned professionals like Neville Southall, Dave Watson, Craig Short, Duncan Ferguson, Barry Horne and Joe Parkinson. It was a British core and they were prepared to go to war every week. That excited Dunne, who relished the combative side of the game that referees facilitated by 'letting a few things go'.

Within a year, however, Dunne could see that things were beginning to change across the Premier League. 'You looked at the style of football that Arsenal were playing at that time and the players that they had to go along with it, they were outstanding players. Some people thought that you can't play like that in England but Arsenal were dominating games and people were trying to follow suit,' remembers Dunne. 'You also had a lot of British managers in the league at the time. And you don't just change your philosophy overnight. It takes time to run through the whole Premier League. But you look at things now and there are not many [traditional] centre forwards around, all of the centre-halves have to be able to play and dribble out from the back. It's been a progression. But for it to be what it is now it had to start somewhere, and credit to Arsène Wenger on making the big changes.'

There would still be individual battles, of course, particularly with the likes of Alan Shearer, Kevin Davies and Emile Heskey, but the game was evolving and the role of the Number 9 changed with it. As Dunne moved on to Manchester City in 2000, he was facing forwards who would drop deep or play wide instead of coming right up against him. Naturally, he had to adjust his own game accordingly.

City too were changing. When Dunne first arrived, City were still playing at the outdated Maine Road stadium and the target was simply to survive in the Premier League. Over the course of the next decade, however, City would emerge as a superpower in club football. 'It's a huge, huge turnaround. It's almost like two different clubs,' says Dunne. 'The Man City who I signed for were known as a yo-yo club, they were up and down every year. So it was about trying to create a stability. And I think the Man City of today wouldn't have been able to become what it has without the stability that we put in place.

'Then the Abu Dhabi [United] Group came in and bought the club [in 2008]. All of a sudden it wasn't about just staying in the league any more, now it was about going to win the league and become the champions of Europe in the future. I think it was on a transfer deadline day when the club was sold and you see all of the different players that they are trying to sign. I think Robinho was the first to come in [for a club-record fee of £32.5 million] and you knew straight away that the expectations had changed. It wasn't going to be a club that settled for second best. How they have worked over the years and produced the club that they have produced is exceptional.'

Part of this development, of course, meant an influx of new players. Dunne, after nearly a decade at the club – and after having won the Man City Player of the Year on four occasions – eventually found himself surplus to requirements. 'When I was there you could see it changing as they were bringing in a lot of players. There is no loyalty in football, it doesn't matter if you're there for two months or twenty years, if they see a better option they'll take it. I was twenty-nine, almost thirty when I left City, so I understood how football works.'

There is no statue of Dunne outside the Etihad Stadium, but he knows that he played his part in the club's history (even helping them get promoted again after they were relegated in his first season there). It is why there is no bitterness about missing out on the glory years that started the year after his departure, with an FA Cup success and a third-place finish in the Premier League.

Dunne moved on to Aston Villa, who reached the League Cup Final in his first year and during his time at the club he saw its Irish contingent grow as he was joined by Shay Given, Ciaran Clark, Enda Stevens, Derrick Williams, Stephen Ireland, Samir Carruthers and Graham Burke, while Robbie Keane stopped by for a short loan spell from LA Galaxy. They were good times. 'I enjoyed my time at Aston Villa. Man City went on to be very successful. So you don't get too attached because you know it can change overnight.'

Sandwiched between his days at Everton, Man City and Aston Villa were eighty caps for Ireland. If he is considered to be one of the best defenders in the first three decades of the Premier League, then his status at international level – at least in the hearts and minds of Irish supporters – is of legendary proportions. There was the 'Moscow Mission', when he smashed his head off the running track in the Luzhniki Stadium and got up again to put in a masterclass of defending. There were important goals, too, big tackles and even bigger performances. He rightly deserves his place in the FAI Hall of Fame.

After a few season with Villa, he joined Queens Park Rangers in the Championship. Dropping down a level didn't deter Dunne from moving to the London club, as he knew that they were on an upward trajectory. 'It was weird because I missed the full season prior to going there [due to injury] and I wasn't sure if I was going to be able to play or not. I think in the end I played something like forty-two out of forty-eight games in the Championship. I loved it, had a great time,' says Dunne.

He played a pivotal role in getting the club promoted to the Premier League. 'Then the following year in the Premier League, the manager [Harry Redknapp] got sacked and the club wanted to go a different way and the dressing room becomes a lot younger than you. It was just a different era, I was a different generation compared to the players coming through. It's mad because you always look at yourself being a young player coming into the dressing room and in the blink of an eye you're thirty-five and you're the old one.'

Dunne has always known when to move on. It is precisely why he won't be spending much time reminiscing about what he did in the past. He would much rather focus on what's next.

14

Stephen Elliott

Manchester City (2003–04), Sunderland (2005–06)

Games Played: 17

Goals Scored: 2

Assists Created: 0

Clean Sheets: 0

Yellow Cards: 0

Red Cards: 0

Wins: 2

Draws: 2

Losses: 13

The ball had just fizzed wide of our post. We collectively exhaled a sigh of relief. It was a warning sign that the pressure being exerted by the opposition was only going to increase. Already trailing by 2-0 with barely twenty minutes played, something had to be done.

As our goalkeeper took his time to first retrieve the ball from the nearby bushes and then place it down for a goal kick, tension hung in the air like a fog cloud. Nobody wanted the ball, because with possession came the responsibility of attempting to get into the other half of the pitch, and that looked to be a great distance away. Too far for any of us to run with it or even kick it that far.

All of a sudden, Stephen Elliott abandoned his position as striker – the one player who could possibly keep the ball in the opposition's half should it ever reach there again. He came all the way back to the edge of our penalty area, on the left side, and began shouting for our goalkeeper to feed him the ball. Everyone was confused: why would we play a goal-kick short? And why would we give it to our striker?

Elliott insisted and so the goalkeeper passed the buck, sorry, passed the ball to him. He took the ball with ease, opened up his body and began to run forward with it. The other team were almost sneering at the audacity of this guy: 'Look at him come at us, thinking that he can actually go somewhere with that ball'. Yet he did. Elliott skipped past their striker with ease, then jinked inside their winger and pushed the ball forward. Suddenly everyone took notice as he was about to do something either magical or foolish.

My cameo role in this involved running alongside Elliott, from my central midfield position, and opening space for him to roam into, almost like a linebacker clearing a route for a running back in American football. I began to shout at my team-mate to pass the ball. He ignored me or maybe didn't hear me. So I began shouting louder, feeling that his charge forward was about to end with an almighty crash and an offload to me would gain us an extra few yards.

Elliott had other things on his mind. He clicked into a higher gear and his pace allowed him to ghost past two more players. He had now crossed the halfway line and the other team raised their warning bell as they each made a charge towards him. Still, I barked out: 'PASS IT; ELLIOTT, PASS IT'. But he was in the zone and my supporting run did not enter into his consciousness.

He slalomed past another player as he moved the ball infield and just as the white lines of the opposition's penalty area appeared, he arched his body slightly backwards before swinging his right leg towards the ball.

Everything seemed to happen in slow motion as the normally heavy leather ball floated through the air. It curled slightly – and at just the right time – to nestle into the top corner of the net, out of reach of their goalkeeper.

It was a goal and what a goal it was.

I stopped on the edge of the area, pretty much out of breath, and said to myself: 'Oh, that's what he was doing.' It was at that moment that I knew that Stephen Elliott would go on to play in the English Premier League.

Okay, that goal was scored for O'Connell's School's Third Year team against a school in Kilkenny or Kildare with whom we would go on to draw. But it was the majestic touches of the ball, the roaring power in his legs, the single-minded focus to take on an entire team and the sublime technique to apply the perfect finish that made it such a special goal. It was similar to George Weah's fantastic solo effort against Verona in 1996 (YouTube it if you haven't seen it), except this was a teenage Dubliner doing it, not an AC Milan superstar.

Within a few months Elliott had signed a contract to join Manchester City. My class-mate and team-mate was going on to bigger things. The Premier League was waiting for him and I was excited for the rest of the world to see what he was capable of.

***

Reconnecting over twenty years later, Elliott has hung up the boots and now focuses on giving young players the chance that was afforded to him through his role as academy director at Darlington.

He is proud of what he achieved in his career, and rightly so. There were Premier League stints with Manchester City and Sunderland, a break-out year in the Championship, some highs at Preston North End and Hearts, as well as one goal in nine senior appearances for the Republic of Ireland.

But, more important, what does he recall of lining out for his school team? 'I remember playing the odd game for the school. We weren't great, were we? But it was a good way of getting out of class. I even played the Gaelic to get out of more classes. But I remember Mr Rice, the science teacher, used to let me away with doing homework if I played well on the football pitch.'

Elliott was always the stand-out player in our school. Whether it was a chaotic game on knee-shredding concrete at lunch-time or double P. E. on Friday afternoons, it was always a case of give him the ball and he would score.

Of course there was a little jealousy involved. I wanted to be as good as he was, not as a striker, but someone whose first touch was perfect, whose runs were always well-timed and whose ability to produce something special seemed so effortless. The difference was that he played for the top schoolboy team in the country in Belvedere and I was a battling midfielder with Kinvara Boys – only about twenty divisions between us.

During school holidays and mid-term breaks, Elliott would always be away in England training – or auditioning – with a big club. For a long time it was Arsenal but then he was gone for good, to Manchester City. Our school team had just lost its main goalscorer but Irish football had gained another great talent. 'Just like most kids, all I wanted to do was play football. I suppose when scouts were knocking on my door I knew that I had something extra. From the age of thirteen, fourteen I had a feeling that I would be going away to England at some stage. Manchester City were the first to offer me a contract and I was happy to sign with them because I felt very comfortable there. There were a few Irish lads there at the time in Whelo [Glenn Whelan], Paddy McCarthy, Stephen Paisley, Brian Murphy and Willo [Flood].'

He may have been comfortable, but his beginnings at the club did not go as expected. 'Believe it or not, I had become too old to play for the youth team and I was thrown in with the first team; having not even trained with the reserve team, it was straight in. There was no training kit for me when I went over to the first team and there was no record of me going in. I was like 'this is a great start'. But I just made a joke of it and the kitman, who I knew from being around Maine Road, fixed me up and gave me number 45, which turned out to be my actual squad number. I literally went from not having any kit to training with Nicolas Anelka, Robbie Fowler and all these boys.

He could well have felt out of his depth, but instead he settled quickly. '[The manager at the time] Kevin Keegan took a liking to me and I was lucky enough to be in and around the first team from Christmas onwards. Then lucky enough that I managed to get on the pitch a couple of times as well. I remember the first time that I was on the bench, it was against Liverpool in Anfield. I was a Liverpool fan growing up so I was loving the experience. In those days we only had five substitutes so I was often one of the players that missed out because we would bring seventeen or eighteen players to each game. I remember Kevin Keegan called the team out and he said that Stuey is on the bench – at the time I had the nickname of Stuey – and I turned around to Joey Barton or Shaun Wright-Phillips and said: "Did he just call my name?" I couldn't believe it. I never got on the pitch but it was a surreal experience.

'I was on the bench a few times after that without getting on and then we played Bolton away at what was then called the Reebok Stadium. I think both Robbie Fowler and Steve McManaman came off and I went on for the last five minutes. It was surreal coming on with them going off with me being a Liverpool fan who idolised these players. It was a great moment and even though it was only a few minutes it seemed to last forever in my mind.'

There would be one more substitute appearance before Elliott made the decision to leave in the summer of 2004. City had offered a two-year extension but he craved more regular first-team football and believed that that could be secured elsewhere. The decision to move wasn't an easy one to make but making tough calls was all part of becoming a professional footballer. 'You have to grow up quick. I moved away on my sixteenth birthday, so I was still a kid. I have kids now, eighteen, sixteen and fifteen, and I'm looking at them thinking that they won't even make their bed never mind moving away from home,' says Elliott. 'When I left City I remember thinking: "I'm making a huge decision here that is going to affect the rest of my life." I just felt that if I stayed at City I might not play regularly and I was nineteen, twenty, so I felt ready to play first-team football.'

A move to Celtic, where Martin O'Neill was in charge, almost happened. But then Elliott met another former Ireland manager in Mick McCarthy, who was leading Sunderland, and was immediately won over. It meant dropping down to the Championship but that didn't matter because the club had ambitions to be among the Premier League elite within a year. And that proved to be the case after Elliott's fifteen goals helped them secure promotion.

That first season at senior level was just bliss. Elliott became an instant fan favourite with the Sunderland crowd as he scored crucial goals and showed why many observers had described him as Ireland's best natural finisher since Robbie Keane.

Unfortunately, that proved to be his best season. It was almost like a long adventure-filled summer that brought adolescence to a closure in the most memorable way before the cruelty of the real world hit hard. As Elliott says himself: 'it wasn't always sunshine and lollipops, but I got to play football for a living so I can't complain'.

There were two goals – two great goals against Manchester United and Newcastle United respectively – in his one Premier League season with Sunderland. With the Number 10 on his back and the club's fans behind him, it should have been a magical year. It wasn't. The Black Cats ran out of lives and suffered relegation. Back to the Championship to start over.

Elliott got back into the groove of playing again but a return of five goals wasn't near good enough for his high standards. Then he joined Wolves and did relatively well in his first season – scoring four times – before injuries started to reduce his momentum to a stop-start pace. It would be that way for the remainder of his career as he made stops at

Preston North End, Norwich City, Hearts, Coventry City, Carlisle United, Shelbourne and Drogheda United. But you won't catch him complaining about being unlucky with injuries, no matter how much they prevented him from reaching greater heights.

'When I was seventeen, when I first went to Man City, I fractured my back and missed the best part of seven months. I was just sitting in the digs, I couldn't move, I couldn't even go to the training ground. So you have to deal with injuries and set-backs. Looking back on my career, I was always managing my body from when I was a young lad. I would never have regrets about whether I could've done more because I always did everything that I had to do and what I was told to do. I was lucky enough to get a good go of it. Okay, not always in the Premier League, but I did play at good levels and played for some really big clubs. I just always look back to when I was a kid in O'Connell's when it was my dream to go on to be a professional player. I did that and I'm proud that I did.'

***

On 16 November 2004, the Republic of Ireland hosted Croatia in an international friendly. I had crammed into the schoolboy section in the old Lansdowne Road with a bottle of warm Coke in my jacket pocket, an Ireland jersey on underneath and a smirk on my face that suggested I knew something that others didn't. That something was the knowledge of just how good Ireland's new striker actually was.

All my friends had grown tired of hearing about my school team games alongside this amazing striker by the time the DART pulled into Lansdowne station. So once I was inside the ground, my propaganda was spread to anyone willing to listen. 'Watch out for the little lad up front alongside Robbie Keane'. 'Yeah, he's with Sunderland. Lethal in front of goal. If Duff can get the service into him, don't be surprised if he scores on his debut.'

While he didn't score in the eighty-five minutes he spent on the pitch, Elliott did me proud. Not that he was playing for me. It was more that his performance suggested that he could mix it with the big lads at this level, which, in turn, gave some form of validation to the propaganda that I had been spouting all day long.

Over the years, I repeated that endorsement whenever I watched Elliott on TV, playing for his clubs. When he scored that smashing goal against Manchester United, I must've repeated 'told ya so' about a million times. I always backed him to be a success, to score goals and to come back from his injuries.

Elliott didn't turn out to be a Premier League star, but he did have his moments when he made people take notice. That was good enough for me. And it was clearly good enough for him.

Still, he should've passed the ball to me all those years ago!

15

Stephen Quinn

Sheffield United (2006–07), Hull City (2013–15)

Games Played: 58

Goals Scored: 3

Assists Created: 5

Clean Sheets: 2

Yellow Cards: 3

Red Cards: 1

Wins: 12

Draws: 13

Losses: 33

Footballers don't cry.

They are programmed to display only two types of emotion: aggression and joy. Anything else will spoil the entertainment for the fans. The loss of a loved one, however, hits harder than any tackle ever can. We want to believe that professional athletes are superhuman. They have to be, we tell ourselves, because they made it when we didn't. But the truth is that they are just the same as us; they bleed, they make mistakes and they cry.

Stephen Quinn was one year into his life as a professional footballer when he wanted to give it up. It wasn't that he found the loan spells in the lower leagues in England with MK Dons and Rotherham United too tough (even if he did get 'kicked around the place'). It was that his mother, Alice, had passed away and he felt lost.

The macho environment that football buries itself in, acting almost like a shield, doesn't allow vulnerability to seep into the dressing room. Quinn knew that when he returned to Sheffield United from the loan stints, but bottling it up didn't make it any easier – especially when he lost his father, John, a few years later.

Quinn opens up about that period of his life, saying: 'That was so hard. When she went I was so young, I was only nineteen. You're trying to grieve and play football. You're out on the pitch when you're sad, you're as low as a snake's belly and the fans are giving you pelters. It was really hard to take, especially as I was going to be heading home to visit her that weekend but then she died during the week. It was hard in my twenties because I was trying to forge a career at a high level in a high-pressure industry but yet trying to deal with the loss of my mum and then, a few years later, my dad.

'I had some bad games, looking back on it now, I was grieving and I probably shouldn't have played. I know mental health is being talked about a lot now but back in 2005, 2006, 2007 you weren't talking about it and I didn't want to talk about it. I knew that if I talked about it I would be left out of the team and I didn't want to be left out of the team. I didn't want to show weakness. I came in at the end of a very physical era, the players were tough men. They wouldn't give you a minute to be sad or a minute to not be confident. I remember Keith Gillespie shouting in my face, "Give me the ball, give me the ball." We had hard men in our team and we had a hard-knock manager in Neil Warnock. It was just a tough school and there was no time for fragility.

'I've got tough skin. I don't like people using the term mental health when it's not there for them [i.e. when they haven't been medically confirmed as being depressed], sometimes you're just sad. I know how hard it can get and that was a tough period, losing Mum and Dad. We're a big family and we've had issues in our family through the years, so it's toughened me. I have thick skin now but, looking back, I was grieving a lot through my twenties.'

Grief is not something that is instantly identifiable from the outside. It may not make a player stumble like concussion can, but it does affect the brain in a similar way: by blurring the focus, tricking the decision-making and narrowing one's ambition.

Quinn played through the pain. He buried himself in the football. One game at a time until he slipped into a flow. It helped that he was being challenged by the demands of the Premier League. He made his debut against Charlton Athletic on 2 December 2006 and then scored, against Aston Villa, in his next game. He was doing okay, even if the weight of loss never quite disappeared.

To have reached that level at all was quite an achievement, or at least Quinn thinks so himself. Only two years earlier he had been on an FAI/ ETB course [a football development course run by the Football Association of Ireland to help young players advance in their careers and also earn a qualification] and training with League of Ireland club St Patrick's Athletic. He always believed that he would make it across the water in England, but it happened more quickly than he expected. One day he was playing snooker in Q's Snooker Club in Clondalkin with St Pat's legend Paul Osam, the next he was being offered a contract by Sheffield United.

Playing football is all he ever wanted to do. He remembers being in primary school when Mrs Cahill would call for the pupils to write a short story about any topic at all. As his class-mates started scribbling about their summer holidays or the funny things that their pet dog got up to, Quinn would detail exactly how his dream of becoming a professional footballer would pan out. He may have been in the Dublin suburb of Clondalkin, but in his mind he could see himself scoring a winning goal in Wembley. Then it would transfer to Lansdowne Road, where he would be representing the Republic of Ireland. It was his favourite story to write. The only story that he wrote. Yet Quinn never treated it like a creative writing exercise. It was more of a career blueprint. He was convinced that he would go on to play in Wembley and pull on the green jersey of his country. It was only a matter of when.

The path had been set in a way for the fiery midfielder, whose shock of flame-red hair made him stand out wherever he went, as his older brother Alan was already forging his way as a footballer in England. It seemed only natural that the younger brother would follow a similar route.

Ironically, the route was almost identical as Quinn moved to the steel city of Sheffield just as Alan joined the Blades from their city rivals Sheffield Wednesday. But it wasn't a case of the little brother pulling on his elder's coat tails; he wanted to learn for himself and become his own man.

'When I went over I wanted to not rely on Alan. I wanted to forge my own pathway and figure out myself what I needed to do. I was just a kid from Dublin. The minute you get off the plane you're fighting for your place because there are lads in the team ahead of you and you're trying to overtake them and take their position. And Alan happened to be one of those players. We're brothers but there was no love lost in training. Alan used to run around with his elbows held high. You're brothers but it's work. We'd have a go at each other, we'd smash each other in tackles, but it's like anybody else. You're determined to win and to do what you can to get into the team.'

From the outside looking in, it may seem like nepotism was at play in Quinn's rise to becoming a Premier League player. But he insists that his break came after a lot of hard grafting. 'For me and Alan to have played professional football at a high level, in the Premier League, looking at it now I think it's an unbelievable feat. For two brothers from a council estate in Dublin to make it that high is some going, because I know how hard it is to try and sustain the level. And anyone who does make it as a professional footballer, hats off to them because people always think, back in the pubs, back at home, "I could've been this, I could've been that." You couldn't have because you didn't. You didn't sacrifice, you didn't do the hard work, you didn't stay away from home, you didn't stay in digs, you didn't stay away from your family, you didn't put the work in day in, day out. There's so many factors and it's miles more than talent. It's so bloody hard.'

The Quinn brothers only shared the pitch once in the Premier League, when Alan was introduced as a substitute late on in the draw with Everton in March 2007. Up to that point, they were rivals competing for the same midfield spot. In fact, Alan came on for Stephen earlier in that season in a loss to Middlesbrough. However, it was the younger sibling who played more games in that 2006–07 season.

Relegation followed at the end of that campaign. The physicality of the Championship became their reality for the next season before Alan left for Ipswich Town. Stephen stayed and got to fulfil the dream of playing at Wembley – only for it to become a bad memory as they lost the play-off final to Burnley.

Quinn stuck around for another few seasons, suffering relegation again as the Yorkshire club dropped into League One. And there would be more Wembley heartbreak as Huddersfield Town denied them in the 2012 play-off final to get back up to the second tier. 'I went through a lot of hurt and loss. From relegation from the Premier League to two play-off final defeats to relegation again to League One and dealing with the loss in my family, it was all loss, loss, loss. I suppose I did mature a lot in those seven years but it was very tough.'

It was time for a change and Hull City came calling in August 2012. 'When I went to Hull, it was like a fresh start. Those three years were the most enjoyable of my career. We got promoted to the Premier League and I got to play alongside lads who became great friends of mine, the likes of Maccer [Paul McShane], Robbie [Brady], Longy [Shane Long] and David Meyler. It was like playing with your mates, we got on so well and loved coming into training every day.'

He had, by that point, likely come through the worst of his grief. 'I was probably over the grieving process. I was towards my late twenties then and

I was comfortable with how I was playing. We got promoted, I got Players' Player of the Year, we got to the FA Cup Final the next year, we got into Europe, it was a good three years at Hull … probably the best of my career.'

Add to that success his eighteen caps for the Republic of Ireland, including a cameo off the bench in the famous win over Italy in Lille during the 2016 European Championships, and Quinn can confidently declare that he made it to the top. He may not have a mantelpiece stacked with trophies and medals, but he has a lifetime of memories to play on repeat in his mind's eye.

At the age of thirty-six, Quinn is still playing. He ended the 2021–22 season in League Two at Mansfield Town, where they lost in another play-off final at Wembley. Yes, again! So he is determined not to end it all with such a stinging defeat. Always searching for the positive outcome, Quinn has learned how to deal with set-backs: by focusing on what is yet to come.

16

Paul McShane

Sunderland (2007–09), Hull City (2009–10, 2013–15)

Games Played: 98

Goals Scored: 2

Assists Created: 0

Clean Sheets: 17

Yellow Cards: 12

Red Cards: 1

Wins: 24

Draws: 23

Losses: 51

'I got to a bit of a "fuck it" moment. Whatever happens, happens.'

It wasn't so much a mid-life crisis, but rather an acceptance that Paul McShane could only be who he is. He had spent his entire career fretting about being somebody different, being some form of perfect. Yet, at the age of thirty, and his playing days seemingly coming to an end, he had found peace within himself.

Suited up in a Manchester United tracksuit – having returned as a coach to the club where he started out in England twenty years before – McShane shares his experiences of becoming a Premier League footballer, surviving for six seasons, up to that moment in 2016 when the thirty-year-old McShane, then playing in the Championship with Reading, suddenly realised that he was ready to accept the player that he was. Life can be funny that way, almost like a postman delivering your most anticipated gift long after your birthday has passed.

Wicklow's finest, McShane has always stood out from the crowd for three distinctive reasons. First, he jokes, his red hair means that he will never blend into a crowd. Second, he played the game with a full-on intensity, as if someone told him that each game was to be his last. And third, he is a gentleman and an incredibly witty character. He may kick you up in the air during a game, but he could have you rolling around in laughter after it.

When it came to football, however, McShane was always deadly serious. Whether he was ripping it up in the Dublin District Schoolboy League (DDSL) with St Joseph's Boys or overpowering the Czech Republic's giant 6ft 8in striker Jan Koller on his Republic of Ireland senior debut in the old Lansdowne Road, he always gave it everything. And that's why Man United signed him up.

He would go on to play in the Premier League with Sunderland and Hull City, coming up just short of 100 games, with his confidence building year on year. There was an impatient side to him, too, that always wanted things yesterday, but mostly he remained focused on simply playing as many games as possible in what he considers to be the best league in the world.

There were times when he doubted whether he belonged. And there were times when he felt that his performances justified his position on the pitch alongside so many superstar players. In fact, there were games when he hassled and harried the big-name players so much that he nullified their superpowers. His aggression was kryptonite to them.

Rewind back to 2004 and he also felt ready to take his chance in the Premier League. Unfortunately, there was quite a queue of defenders in front of him at Man United so he needed to find an alternative route. A loan spell in the Championship with Brighton & Hove Albion changed everything.

McShane explains: 'I felt myself that I should've got a chance before I went out on loan or I should've had at least a debut. I saw players around me getting debuts and I felt that it should've been me. So I had this thing in me going, 'I'm going to leave here and make a career for myself because I can't wait around forever to get that Man United first-team debut. So when I went out on loan to Brighton, I knew I was playing well, I was clocking up the games and I could see people around my age at United that weren't playing regular first-team football. So, in my head, I was thinking that when I go back to Man United, if I'm not with the first team every day I'm going to have to leave the club and try to make a career for myself elsewhere.'

Breaking in at Man United was no easy feat at that time, however. 'The odds were stacked against me because at the time Man United were probably the best in the world. I made that decision myself. I had a year left on my contract and I handed in a transfer request because I didn't want to play in the reserves for a year. I knew my stock was high out there in the Football League so I needed to kick on with my career.'

Saying that, leaving one of the giants of the Premier League was not an easy decision. 'You have to weigh up the situation and understand the circumstances around it. Sometimes a player can leave too early. In my case I definitely needed to go. When you look back, playing for United at the time was Rio Ferdinand, Nemanja Vidic, Wes Brown, John O'Shea, then around my age you had Gerard Piqué, Jonny Evans, Ryan Shawcross, so it was really competitive. I think it was the right decision for me to leave. Sometimes you have to be brave and roll the dice a little bit.'

When he left Old Trafford behind, there was a burning desire within him to prove people wrong. He wanted to show that he could compete against the best at the top level. Soon enough, he was testing himself at the top table. 'The Premier League came earlier than I expected. When I left Man United I signed for West Brom and we got beaten in the play-off final to go to the Premier League and Sunderland came in for me. I couldn't wait to go and to play under Roy [Keane] as manager. It was another opportunity that I jumped at.'

Not that it was all plain sailing. 'It was a bit of a whirlwind. I was still learning as a defender and as a young defender you make mistakes at times. I was at the elite level, in the Premier League and at international, so I was highly scrutinised. Some games it was tough to take if you were getting criticised, but that is part of the game. It helped me grow as a player and as a person.'

McShane's time in the north-east of England with Sunderland had more ups and downs than a game of snakes and ladders. There were fantastic highs but also crushing lows. Yet behind the scenes, there was always an upbeat atmosphere due to the camaraderie among the ten Irish players in the first-team squad. 'As Irish lads, we were always a tight group. I remember that we always played head tennis in the mornings in the indoor centre at the training ground. The odd English or Scottish lad would be thrown in. We were using it to improve ourselves but also to have a bit of craic as well.'

Were any of the Irish lads ever accused of being a teacher's pet with Roy?

'No. I think we got it worse, to be honest. I think he felt that he could hammer us even more because he knew Irish people and how we would react to it all.'

Just like Keane's style of management, the Premier League could be unforgiving. McShane could feel the weight of expectation long before even arriving at a stadium on match day. He says: 'Just the whole build-up around games, obviously the coverage is a lot more, you could feel the atmosphere around games, the quality of the players, the speed of the players and I quickly realised that any mistake is pretty much punished. Your concentration levels would have to go up another notch when you played in the Premier League because of the quality there and the strikers that you are up against are the best in the world. It can be mentally draining when you're so up against it and you're fighting for every point. You're tested with everything that you've got.'

As McShane had wanted when starting out, he was now testing himself against the very best. 'It's elite. It's the highest level that you can play in. There are top leagues out there but the Premier League is relentless.' Some days went better than others. 'I remember playing against Fernando Torres when he was at Liverpool, when he was on fire. I was always confident going into games and felt like I could deal with players but in that game I thought: "This fella is unreal." I couldn't get near him, I didn't know what to do to stop him. He had everything: he was quick, he was skilful, he was good in the air, he was aggressive. So I couldn't really impose myself on him … usually I'd try to get close, try to unsettle them or rag doll them a bit but I couldn't get anywhere near him. I remember thinking that I just wanted the game to be over.'

As a defender, McShane knew that he had to take a chance at times. In order to stop certain strikers he had to adopt different tactics. And it was the same with opponents trying different things to outsmart him. One of those tactics was the mind games that could be described as 'banter' but were clearly used to throw someone's focus off their job at hand. 'The biggest one for that was Craig Bellamy. I played against him a few times and we ended up getting on quite well actually. But he would wind you up,' says McShane. 'The first time I didn't want to get involved, I didn't want to play him at his own game, but I found a way to get around him. I'd always give a little bit back to him but in a different way to how he would do it. We had a few battles over the years.'

Did it ever happen with Irish players when he came up against them in league games?

'Always in the back of my mind there would be an element of respect that I would have for the Irish players. I knew that they had been on the same journey that I had been on. I'd always try to avoid getting involved with anyone that was Irish because it didn't feel right, it felt like I had a loyalty to them. But if an Irish player got involved with me with verbals I'd be quite insulted. I wouldn't be angry but really sad. I would be thinking that that's not right. We're supposed to be together and have each other's backs. Sometimes it would upset me if someone said something. It only happened a couple of times, but it was disappointing when it did.'

The lighter side of the Premier League is something that McShane played a part in cultivating at both Sunderland and, later, at Hull City. A very public example was when his Hull team-mates mocked their own manager, Phil Brown, with a goal celebration that reflected back on a bizarre team talk that he put them through on the pitch at half-time a year earlier following an abysmal first-half.

'That was funny. I was on the pitch when Phil did the team talk. Then the following season I just had a brainwave the night before a game that this would be a great celebration if we done it. I told the lads on the bus going over to Manchester and we had an agreement that we would do it, but only if it was an equaliser or a winner. It worked perfectly that Jimmy [Bullard] scored a penalty and we did it. It worked great. It was nearly in the exact same spot as the year before when Phil was telling us off. The manager didn't really say anything, he just laughed it off.'

After finishing up with Hull in 2015, McShane dropped down a division to link up with Reading for four seasons, having his 'fuck it' epiphany while being coached by former Man United defender Jaap Stam. He played with the freedom of that realisation that he could only be who he is during the rest of his time at Reading, and at Rochdale in League One, where he finished his playing days.

Then an unexpected move – back to Man United as a player/coach for their Under-23s. Unsurprisingly, McShane has made the most of the opportunity at his former club by helping out with the Under-14s, Under-15s, Under-16s and Under-18s. He has created a 'defenders' union', whereby he identifies clips from specific games and brings the rookier defenders together to debate and analyse them. It is part of their education but also part of his in the role of coach.

A natural leader, McShane has a lot of the attributes required to be a coach at an elite level. Typical of his ambition, however, he would like to aim a little higher. 'The long-term goal is to go into management. But you just don't know what happens, really. In the back of my mind I'm always thinking that I'd like to manage a club but at the moment I'm just focusing on trying to help the players in the academy and to help them make careers for themselves. So being a coach or mentor to those lads and also learning the trade. I think you can learn a lot in academies before you go into a first team and try to manage.

'I'm just on a journey now. Basically I'm back to my apprentice days, but in the coaching world. I'm just trying to learn and improve every day. It's mad that I've ended up back at Man United. I was lucky, to be honest. It was right place, right time, and it has been a great place for me to learn as a coach.'

No longer weighed down by things he cannot control, McShane is content with what he achieved as a player yet determined to be the best coach/manager that he can be.

17

Stephen Kelly

Tottenham Hotspur (2003–06), Birmingham City (2007–08),
Stoke City (2008–09), Fulham (2009–13), Reading (2013)

Games Played: 141

Goals Scored: 2

Assists Created: 0

Clean Sheets: 18

Yellow Cards: 7

Red Cards: 0

Wins: 39

Draws: 35

Losses: 67

Training had just finished at Tottenham Hotspur's old training ground in Chigwell. Stephen Kelly wiped away sweat from his forehead and slugged from a bottle of water. His legs felt heavy and his ribcage heaved as his lungs attempted to suck in more oxygen. He was looking forward to a cold shower and a hot meal. Then the shadow of Chris Hughton appeared in front of him. Training was not over yet. Or at least, not for eighteen-year-old Kelly. He was being kept after class for extra lessons, signalled by Hughton's quietly said three words: 'You're with me.'

At the time, Kelly was an eager young centre-back with his sights set on breaking into the first-team squad. Hughton saw a different pathway for him and wanted to mould the Dubliner into a fearless full-back who could play on either side of the pitch. Hughton, a former Republic of Ireland international, was first-team coach at Tottenham and was known for being ahead of his generation in how he coached. Among the first coaches in England to earn the UEFA Pro Licence – the highest coaching qualification in professional football – he demanded a lot from players but knew how to get the best out of them. And Kelly was an attentive student.

Once the cones were put in place, Hughton would fire balls at Kelly to test his reaction speed, his balance and his control of the ball. They would practise how he would pass the ball into a striker from a defensive position – the strike of the ball, the weight of the pass, the angle of the pass. Again and again, they would practise this before graduating to the next discipline.

'Chris was probably the biggest influence on me. He was a right-footed left-back in his career and I was comfortable using both feet, so he was showing me how when you cut inside on your right foot it opens up the pitch. So it's not a bad thing playing on the opposite side because you can use your strong foot and see a bigger picture. There were things like that we would work on quite regularly. He was massive in how I went from being a centre-back to a full-back. I was happy to stay back and do it so there was never an issue with it, whereas some of the other players probably weren't as interested. He obviously saw something in me that he thought I needed work on to get to the Premier League level. It was by working with Chris that I was able to progress into the first team. As a young player you have to take something like that with both hands, you don't turn an opportunity like that down. I think as you get older as a player you probably feel that you don't need it but I was someone who was receptive to it and I think Chris spotted that in me.'

In one sense, it was madness that Kelly was being persuaded to pursue a career at full-back considering fellow Irishman Stephen Carr was well established in the right-back spot at the club. In fact, Carr had just been voted onto the PFA Premier League Team of the Year. So Kelly was being prepped to challenge not just a Republic of Ireland international who was a crowd favourite at Spurs, but also someone who was among the best full-backs in the Premier League.

However, Hughton was impressed by Kelly's athleticism and felt that he possessed the kind of speed required to excel in the modern game. While Kelly had always played at centre-back – even operating there on his first loan spell with Southend United – he was ultimately convinced by Hughton's vision for where his career could go as a full-back.

Glenn Hoddle was the Tottenham manager then and he liked what he saw in Kelly, especially during the bounce games on Friday mornings when the youth team would take on the first team. The youth team were meant to be there to play in the style of Tottenham's next opponent, but, naturally, it turned into a scrappy affair with young players desperate to catch the manager's eye. Kelly recalls: 'I have memories of smashing Les Ferdinand in a tackle. I was thinking "Oh God, what have I just done?" but he was a senior pro and took it well. There was a bit of banter with the lads as this young kid had just smashed into him. He patted me on the back, as if to say keep it going, but then a few minutes later he was smashing me with an elbow. That was all part of it.'

How a young player responds to a challenge will always determine whether they make it or not in the professional game. Kelly learned that early on. He discovered that respect is earned and not given out by senior players. 'I remember I was eighteen in my first pre-season with Spurs, we were in La Manga, and we were doing running on a golf course. This was when you would do running until you got sick. We used to run from the tee box to the green on every hole at seven in the morning. I was in a group with a few of the older pros. The management staff want you to beat them because you are the younger player but the older pros don't want you showing them up, so they are shouting at you and giving you a bit of abuse saying "get back here" or whatever. I remember Jamie Redknapp being like that but then when we got to the end of the run he said: "Don't be listening to that, make sure you show us what you can do. Don't hold back because a senior pro tells you to because you will get more respect by beating them." That always stuck with me.'

Kelly made his Tottenham debut in 2003, when David Pleat was the interim manager after Hoddle, and he would feature in two seasons before moving to Birmingham City in search of regular game-time. That meant dropping down a division to the Championship but he was back in the Premier League within a year after achieving promotion. Unfortunately, the Blues lasted only one season in the top tier before suffering relegation.

Kelly stayed for one more year before Fulham brought him back to London. This was when he played some of his best football and it was hardly a coincidence that it happened within a changing room that had the right balance between respect, a competitive edge and a desire to win at all costs. Always someone who looks on the bright side of life, Kelly can testify as to how harmony within a squad is one of the unheralded qualities that all teams need.

Players who are motivated by individual rewards can tear a squad apart as teamwork becomes just another clichéd slogan painted on the wall that they bypass without a second glance. Kelly, though, insists that those types of character are sniffed out quickly within the Premier League environment. 'Respecting each other and what you contribute are key. A lot of it is respecting the other guy in the changing room and for him to respect what you do, that then builds a bond between the players. Then you have time-keeping and not turning up late for things. It's the players that don't do that who fall out of the team. If you have a standard set in your changing room then the players who don't follow it don't tend to last very long.'

While the players set the standard within the changing room, it is the manager who dictates the tone everywhere else. It comes down to the values and authority of one man to ensure that a team acts in the right manner long before they have crossed the white line to step onto a football pitch. If that atmosphere isn't right in the training ground, on the team bus, on their fancy chartered flights, in the five-star hotels and in their team meetings, their chances of becoming a successful team are slim.

A good captain can help with that, but they have their own performances to worry about. Every general needs a reliable lieutenant but they are the ones still charged with plotting the tactics and making the big decisions. 'Sometimes you had quiet captains, like Ledley [King, at Tottenham Hotspur], who was so quiet but every time he went onto the pitch you knew that he was going to be exceptional. That was my favourite type of leader, they did it with their feet. They didn't have to be shouting all over the place. The ones who are consistent in how they perform and the standards they hold, they are the ones you want to follow and play with.

'On managers, I've had some who just didn't take any nonsense. That in itself was brilliant as a player because you knew whoever it was they wouldn't get away with doing things wrong. The manager sets the tone for how he wants things to be. Hodgson was like that. He was aggressive and opinionated and intelligent and he knew what he wanted. If you didn't do things the way he wanted then you wouldn't be part of the team. At Fulham we had a great group of players who all fed into that attitude and mindset, so it's no surprise that we ended up reaching the Europa League Final.'

Fulham lost that final to Atletico Madrid in May 2010.

Even Kelly's decision to remodel himself as a full-back paid off at club level, particularly during his spells with Birmingham City, Fulham and Reading. It was quite another thing in the international arena, however, as ahead of him in the pecking order at right-back were Stephen Carr, Steve Finnan, John O'Shea, Kevin Foley and, later, Seamus Coleman. Despite this, he did collect thirty-nine senior caps, lead the team out for an international friendly against Uruguay at the Aviva Stadium and make the squad for Euro 2012 (without ever getting onto the pitch). And former

Ireland manager Giovanni Trapattoni did even use him in his old centre-back position at times. But the decision to become a full-back probably held him back at international level.

'It's been our strongest position for the last fifty years. It's ridiculous when you list out all of the different names. When I came into the Ireland team, we had full-backs in the Premier League Team of the Year for something like seven years in a row. The fact that I was able to get into the Irish team with that level of competition probably says a lot about my character and how determined I was to succeed. If you want to be the best then you have to try to compete with those types of players. You can say that I was unfortunate to come through in the era that I did but you just have to make the most of it and I'm extremely proud to have represented my country and captained my country.'

Looking back on his club career, however, he doesn't necessarily count himself lucky to have been one of the Irish players to have featured in the Premier League because he feels that he worked hard to earn that right. And in a funny way it all links back to those sessions with Hughton. If the former Ireland international – who would go on to manage Newcastle United, Norwich City and Brighton & Hove Albion in the Premier League – had not given his time to Kelly, his career might have gone down a different path altogether. Kelly thinks about how his Premier League experience is a positive one, in large part because he was given the confidence and coaching to make it happen that way.

18

John O'Shea

Manchester United (2001–2011), Sunderland (2011–18)

Games Played: 445

Goals Scored: 13

Assists Created: 13

Clean Sheets: 115

Yellow Cards: 34

Red Cards: 1

Wins: 218

Draws: 105

Losses: 122

Honours: Premier League (5)

'I don't think you just become a leader. You can't wake up one morning and say: "Right, now I'm going to be a leader." I think it is something that's in you, that you're born with, and which develops. Some people have that character, that personality and it comes naturally. You can't force it. It has to be authentic and natural. Innate. It comes from you, your early years, your attitude as an adolescent, how you are with a group and as the one who influences things.'

Didier Deschamps, France World Cup-winning captain and manager

John O'Shea is a leader. He leads when nobody is watching. He leads when a global audience are tracking his every move. He leads for the right reasons and to achieve positive outcomes.

Gentleman John. A Waterford native, he could have pursued a successful career in business, if his school reports were anything to go by. Celtic FC were keen to get him over to Glasgow as early as possible to help develop his footballing skills. O'Shea, though, insisted that they wait so that he could complete his Leaving Certificate exams.

The glorious summer of 1998 then followed and he did end up in Scotland, but with the Republic of Ireland Under-16s as they defied all expectations to win the UEFA Under-16 European Championships. O'Shea played so well in that tournament that Manchester United made a move for him.

Never one to rush into anything, O'Shea took his time before choosing United over Celtic. That's what leaders do, they make difficult decisions and justify them. Within a year at the club, he had made his debut in a League Cup game on 13 October 1999, aged just seventeen, and started on a journey that would see him enjoy tremendous success.

Twinned with his rise up the ranks at one of the most powerful clubs in world football was the forging of a stellar international career with Ireland at senior level. He captained the team for the first time, against Serbia, in 2012 and would go on to join the exclusive centurion club with 118 caps in total.

Spells with Sunderland and Reading would follow his twelve-year stint at Man United, and it became a regular thing to see the captain's armband hugging his left bicep. Always a leader, always looking to make a difference.

During his time as Sunderland captain, O'Shea's role as a leader was tested on a daily basis as the club gradually allowed complacency to seep into the steelwork that held up the Stadium of Light. As the team slipped into the Premier League's dreaded relegation zone and financial auditors circled like hawks eyeing an easy prey, it was O'Shea who had to be their leader. Why that particular burden fell on the veteran defender had as much to do with the fact that nine different men rotated in and out of the manager's office during that period as it did with his own ability to bring the best out in people.

In his final season, when the Black Cats finally ran out of luck and dropped out of the Premier League, the Netflix cameras were present to capture the gritty reality of a club on the decline for a series called *Sunderland Till I Die*. O'Shea pops up infrequently throughout, but in the final episode we get a glimpse of the type of leader he is.

With staff visibly upset about the future of the club, and their jobs, O'Shea steps through a door from the players' canteen to embrace the cook, Joyce, with a hug and some reassuring words. He then clasps hands with two other staff members in a sign of respect and promises to return the following week to say a proper goodbye. The season is over and O'Shea is set to move on, but you can be sure that he kept that promise.

It is a very real moment in a TV series that shows professional football to be a cruel industry when results are not achieved on the pitch. O'Shea, though, displays the type of humility that we all hope to find in the leaders who enter our lives. Ask around and people who have encountered O'Shea will beam about his ability to be whatever someone needs him to be at any given moment. If they need someone to display courage and put their body on the line in order to defend others, he will do it. If they need someone to offer advice or encouragement to lift morale, he will do it. If they need someone to just be there when life gets tough, he will do it. So make no mistake, that scene at Sunderland was definitely not for the cameras.

O'Shea's emergence as a leader has everything to do with the kindness, discipline, trust and responsibility instilled in him by his family, school teachers at De La Salle, football coaches at Ferrybank and Waterford Bohemians, Brian Kerr and Noel O'Reilly with Ireland underage squads and the countless number of team-mates and coaches at Manchester United who helped the mannerly boy become a respectful man.

An important period in the defender's maturation was when United sent him out on loan to Belgium with Royal Antwerp shortly after he signed with the club. He had already completed a short spell with Bournemouth in the lower leagues, but this was an altogether different challenge. Take someone out of their comfort zone and you will see who they truly are.

'On the outside looking in everyone was thinking that's me finished at United,' says O'Shea of the move to Belgium's second-largest city. 'Young lads maybe stay too long at clubs, at a level that is probably too easy for them. The sooner they can get that competitive first-team football under their belt, to see if they can cope with it with teams looking to survive in leagues. You have to understand what real football is all about. When you are younger and don't have your own kids yet, you're fully focused on yourself so you have to get why games really matter in terms of promotion, relegation. You quickly grow up.'

O'Shea shared a flat with United club-mate Jimmy Davis. They were young men eager to play football but forced to figure everything else out for themselves, such as cooking their own meals. 'I remember a few phone calls back home to get some instructions on certain things, but then you get the hang of it. These are skills that stay with you. I'm no Masterchef but I can do a few bits,' laughs O'Shea.

The spell in Belgium proved to be difficult for Davis, who was homesick and didn't play as many games as O'Shea. That was an early test of O'Shea's leadership qualities, as it became his responsibility to keep his team-mate motivated.

When they eventually returned to United, both were on the fringes of the first-team squad and tipped by many to forge bright futures in the game. O'Shea made the breakthrough first, while Davis went back out on loan – this time to Swindon Town. A talented midfielder, Davis was keen to get going with his career and agreed to join Watford on a season-long loan in the following season. Tragically, he died in a car crash on his way to his first game with the club.

The reality of life came into focus for O'Shea. Not only did he see a friend pass away at the age of twenty-one but the route to the first team at

United looked to be impenetrable. Sir Alex Ferguson's team had just won the Premier League, FA Cup and UEFA Champions League, and on top of that they had just signed France international Mikael Silvestre to add to a defensive unit that already included Gary Neville, Denis Irwin, Jaap Stam, Ronny Johnson, Henning Berg, David May and Phil Neville. Oh, and there was also competition from fellow rookies Wes Brown, John Curtis, Danny Higginbotham and Michael Clegg.

O'Shea recalls: 'I remember people saying "you'll get in the team ahead of this player or that player" but I was thinking: do these people realise how good these players are that they are talking about? The first full season that I joined was the treble-winning season and you're thinking that you're doing okay and people are saying nice things about you but you realise that you have so far to go. I made my debut in 1999 but I didn't properly get into the first-team squad, or the dressing room, until around 2001. The season before I travelled a bit with the first team but that was more so because the manager, Sir Alex Ferguson, always brought a younger player along just to experience what it was like. That was to see what went into travelling away from home, how the players prepare and, ultimately, how they perform on the pitch.'

O'Shea made his Premier League debut in the 2001–02 season and did well enough to convince Ferguson that he had potential. From the next season on, he would be part of the first-team squad and there was no shortage of leaders to learn from. The main man to turn to was the captain, Roy Keane.

'In terms of driving a dressing room, driving a demanding culture of the quality we need, the challenges we are going to face, because teams are wanting to beat you all of the time and that is something we loved, we had someone like Roy leading it,' he says. 'People forget about Roy's quality too. They talk about him being a captain and a leader but when it came to his touch, his passing, he would be as good as anybody. When we played small-sided games in training it was more often than not Roy who was the stand-out player.'

Being appreciated for your skills was something that O'Shea would become known for as his career at United progressed. Actually, his versatility was a regular topic for debate amongst the club's supporters, with some feeling that he needed to lock down one position, while others argued for the advantages of being able to slot in anywhere. And he did just that, by playing in every position for the Red Devils. Yes, including goalkeeper!

'Primarily, even when I went out on loan, I would have been centre-back. But you soon realise the competition you have,' explains O'Shea. 'When I was younger I played in midfield, I played right wing, I played right back, so I knew that I could do a job in lots of positions. When you were called upon you had to be ready.'

Some of the positions he was asked to play did surprise him, however. 'It definitely was a shock when I was asked to play left-back by the manager. But that is when it goes back to your education. In the first year that I joined the club I was practising on improving my weaknesses, which was working a couple of days a week on my left foot to try and make it as close to my right foot, my stronger foot. That was able to get me into the team. It helped me to cope with the demands of games and different players that I would come up against. But I was getting an unbelievable education in training, in terms of the players I was facing and having to mark.'

So what about that cameo between the posts? It was February 2007 and United were on their way to recording a comfortable win over Tottenham Hotspur in a Premier League game when goalkeeper Edwin van der Sar had to go off with a broken nose. With all their substitutions already made, United needed an outfield player to take over as a makeshift goalkeeper.

O'Shea volunteered for the role and one of his first actions was to rush from his goal line to deny compatriot Robbie Keane a goalscoring opportunity. 'I knew what a finisher [Keane] was, never mind how sharp he was, so I had to catch him by surprise. People forget the scoreline in the game at that time, we were 4-0 up so the pressure was kind of off,' says O'Shea. 'It's funny looking at some of the clips. I was on a UEFA course and Julio Cesar, the former Brazil goalkeeper, and Edwin van der Sar, the former Man United and Netherlands goalkeeper, were speaking to us. Someone was saying to Julio Cesar that I had played in goal and then someone showed him the clip. He thought it was hilarious. He said: "interesting technique".'

Perhaps, as with many Irish players, the Gaelic football background may have played a part in O'Shea adapting so well to the role. 'The manager would have been aware that I did play Gaelic as a young lad, but at the time he was more concerned how Edwin was, he didn't mind who was going to go in goal. Rio [Ferdinand] fancied it but I told Gaz [Gary Neville] that I had played Gaelic and he eventually went over to the manager to say: "Stick Sheazy in, he's played a bit of Gaelic." The manager went with it then.'

By that stage, O'Shea was an established member of the United dressing room, with a few Premier League winners' medals in his cabinet at home. But that integration didn't happen by chance. He admits that he had a 'good few people keeping any eye out for me', including fellow Irishmen Roy Keane and Denis Irwin. So whenever an Irish kid arrived at the club – whether that was at United or later on with Sunderland – he would make sure that he was paying it forward and doing what he could to aid their pursuit of a Premier League breakthrough.

'It's about needing that bit of luck, but it's also about being ready to use that luck when that opportunity arrives. Generally it comes when a player is injured. So you're just trying to make them relax because you remember when you were there yourself,' reveals O'Shea. 'It was a bit of an ordeal for different kids. You might have been leaving home for the first time. Some kids were going home every chance they got, while other kids got used to it very quickly. You would go out of your way to ask how they are settling in, if they were going to sign or just coming in on trial. You get a chance to watch them play in games when you could. That emotional attachment would grow as soon as you knew they were signing at the club.

'I remember Eddie Nolan coming over to [Manchester] United and then he ended up signing for Blackburn Rovers. You just keep an eye on their careers from that point going forward. You always tried to give advice where you could. Generally it was the Dublin lads who were a bit more homesick, but ah no, clubs realised that and helped them out. Unfortunately you do have to sacrifice not seeing friends and family as much if you are to fully focus on the demands of becoming a full-time professional.'

Scaling the heights of professional football is something that O'Shea was able to do with United – winning the Premier League (five times), FA Cup, League Cup, UEFA Champions League and FIFA Club World Cup – and with Ireland, where he featured in two UEFA European Championship tournaments. Yet he sought out an altogether different challenge by leaving Old Trafford behind to join Sunderland – a club that had a yo-yo existence in the Premier League when he arrived on Wearside in 2011.

'Leadership requires two things: a vision of the world that does not yet exist and the ability to communicate it.'

Simon Sinek, author and inspirational speaker

O'Shea explains the move: 'The year I joined Sunderland they had just finished tenth in the Premier League. You know that they are not going to be challenging for the title but they are more than mixing it in the Premier League. They were more than competitive and getting amazing support, so you are going to that challenge of can you get to a cup final or win a cup. And we nearly did that when we got to the League Cup Final in 2014, the time we played Man City.'

His time at Sunderland, however, was mostly spent at the other end of the league to which he was accustomed. 'It ended up being a challenge of scrapping to fight to stay in the league. That gave me a whole new side of things ... of managers getting sacked, rotation of squads and players, turnover of players ... it was incredible. In terms of learning about football and what goes on, the time at Sunderland would have been more beneficial to me going forward in a coaching and managerial career.'

Whether it was deliberate or not, O'Shea's decision to join Sunderland was clearly an example of someone embracing a leadership role. Sure, he took over as team captain, but he also became more than that, someone who administrative, operational, technical and support staff leaned on. He was going above and beyond the call of duty. But it felt natural to him.

'You know the people behind the scenes at the club, the staff you're working with and I knew going there what the club meant to people, so it was very educational to see how the club was run and how it reacted to the challenges,' says O'Shea. 'As a captain, you have to understand the group of players you are working with. At the time we had such a turnover of players. Every time the transfer window came around there were five or six players going out and five or six players coming in. So you have to create that atmosphere in the dressing room that people buy into.

'Then there is the staff. Whether it is the kit men, the physios, you are trying to keep them upbeat because we were in so many relegation scraps that we needed people to go again. You are constantly trying to lift the atmosphere. Lots of people at the time meant well, but it was crazy. At the end of the day, we all had contracts, we were getting paid well and, for me, it was always a case of doing a job that you love. So you should be doing your best to succeed. Even when it did go right at times, like when Sam Allardyce came in and we avoided relegation. It looked like Big Sam was the perfect fit for Sunderland. But then England come in and take him to be their manager. So it felt like every time we did do well, something else came around the corner to upset the apple cart. And it can be tough to turn it back around.'

O'Shea clearly learned much from his time at Sunderland. 'I think what's key, not just in football but in business, is the environment that you create. People want to be challenged, people need to be challenged, but it's learning how to speak to certain people and how to motivate them. That's the mindset you need, especially in football. You're not always going to get the best out of everyone but the more chances you have of keeping them positive, keeping them engaged and making them feel special in any way you can, then that is going to be a huge part of any successful team.'

O'Shea stuck around for one more year following Sunderland's relegation from the Premier League in 2017, attempting to lead them back up at the first attempt. It wasn't to be. There were simply too many factors beyond his control. That was a lesson in leadership too: knowing when to step away.

He would play on for one final season, with Reading, before transitioning into coaching. The start of a second career excited him. It would allow him to use the 'education' that he had absorbed as a player and put it into practice as a coach. All by doing it his way.

Typical of the man, O'Shea double-jobbed for a couple of years as first-team coach at Reading and assistant coach with the Ireland Under-21s. With his thirst for knowledge not quenched, he then pursued his UEFA Pro Licence (the highest qualification in coaching) and enrolled in UEFA's Executive Masters for International Players course.

The ambition is to test himself as a football manager, preferably in the Premier League, but he is willing to work hard to earn the chance to reach what he calls the 'elite level'. He certainly has the leadership part sorted.

19
David Meyler

Sunderland (2009–12), Hull City (2013–15, 2013–17)

Games Played: 103

Goals Scored: 4

Assists Created: 2

Clean Sheets: 11

Yellow Cards: 23

Red Cards: 2

Wins: 27

Draws: 29

Losses: 47

Here ... d'ya see it? The 'This Is Anfield' sign? It's a lot shinier than I thought it would be. Think about the number of legendary players who have touched it. The history in this place is unreal. Not sure if I should touch it ... that's for the Liverpool lads, isn't it? Maybe I could sneak it now before anybody sees or just do it naturally like everyone else on the way out of the tunnel.

Ah here they come, the lads. There's Stevie G, Suarez, Coutinho, Sterling. Alright Hendo lad! Good to see ya, catch up after, yeah? Great to see my old mate. Jaysus, that Liverpool team is big. We'll need to be up for it today.

Listen to that, lads, what an atmosphere. I know it's not for me but I'll give the fans a little bualadh bos *anyway. Sure it would be rude not to. What a place this is … Anfield. I've always dreamed of playing here. Now let's get stuck in!*

To be inside the mind of David Meyler when coming out of the tunnel against the club he supported throughout his boyhood must have been a wonderful thing. He has never hidden his love for Liverpool FC, so much so that it wouldn't be a surprise if he had a red jersey on underneath his own team's uniform when coming up against them.

Most professional footballers disconnect, at least emotionally, from the team that they supported in their youth – unless they go on to play for them. They have got a job to do and that may require doing everything they can to beat the team whose posters lined their bedroom walls. It's not easy to do, but it's part of the game.

Meyler was fully aware of that when he lined out in the Premier League with both Sunderland and Hull City. Except he couldn't help himself. 'When the fixture list came out, I was always like: when are we playing Liverpool at Anfield? This is the shit you dream of as a kid. I was a Liverpool supporter, I had a Gerrard top with seventeen on the back and now I'm going up against him. I'll never forget that, the first time I played at Anfield. They are singing "You'll Never Walk Alone" and I was singing it too, not out loud. It was only after the game that Jordan [Henderson] said to me that [Steven] Gerrard said to him, "is he a Liverpool fan?" And he said that he saw me mumbling the words at the start. I was a kid living in a fantasy world. And I hate when football players lose sight of that. This everything you've dreamed of and it's what it's all about.'

Meyler is a fascinating person to engage with on football. He has the experience of someone who has been there and done it in the big games. But he has also never lost the enthusiasm that made him fall in love with the world's most popular sport when he was growing up in Cork. Add to that a scary ability to recall statistics, razor-sharp wit and a fondness for turning casual conversations into animated debates. You've been warned, take Meyler on in a discussion on football and expect to cancel your plans for the afternoon.

When the topic of the Premier League comes up, Meyler continually criss-crosses it with international football. Clearly passionate to have represented the Republic of Ireland, he mentions his time in a green (and sometimes white) jersey quite a lot because he sees a symmetry with his experiences at Sunderland and Hull City. It is too easy to describe it as an underdog complex because there are many layers to it, but Meyler admits that his club and country memories feel twinned because of the style of play, the level of ambition and the hard work that was involved.

It is why he never took his time in the Premier League for granted. For starters, he didn't go through the academy route as he was playing in the League of Ireland with Cork City when Sunderland came calling. Second, he suffered a couple of long-term injuries early on in his professional career to put life into perspective. And, finally, he came from a grounded family background.

'My dad is my biggest fan but the same time is my biggest critic. He said that I was built for away games,' says Meyler. 'If you think about the best games that I played for Ireland ... we're away to Germany, Seamus [Coleman] is out injured, who can we stick at right-back who we know will give us everything? Martin [O'Neill] sticks me out there. Wales away, Martin had told me that I was going to start and be captain.

His attitude was also a positive, he knew. 'The night before the [Wales] game, we were in the snack room and Martin says to me that there is talk of them turning the anthem off and they are going to sing it a cappella. He said, what do you think? I said: "I couldn't give a shit what they do." In my mind I was so focused on us. It was similar to before the Denmark game, when we got hammered [1-5 at the Aviva in a play-off to reach the 2018 World Cup in Russia], Seamus had a go off me because I had said something along the lines of "they don't have as much character and heart as us". Seamus said that we were giving them ammunition but I believed so much in myself and the team, the manager, the people we had around, the staff, I wouldn't have changed anyone.'

He was passionate about his national side, even when he wasn't in the squad. Meyler tells a story of how an injury picked up in Ireland training in 2015 – courtesy of a thunderous challenge from Marc Wilson – meant that he had to watch the Euro 2016 qualifying play-off first leg against Bosnia and Herzegovina in his local pub. Well, he didn't have to choose that location, but it felt apt as all he wanted to do was support his nation. He recalls people looking at him oddly and muttering softly as Meyler jumped around and screamed like a normal fan. He overheard someone say 'It's like he's one of us.'

He was. And always will be.

While that passion for supporting his country is understandable, Meyler feels a similar sort of pride should burn inside every player fortunate enough to have made it to the Premier League. 'I think people lose a bit of love for it,' says Meyler of the modern-day footballer. 'Don't get me wrong, professional football is a cut-throat business – it's ridiculous and horrible. But you also have to pinch yourself and remind yourself of why you do it … it's because you fell in love playing football with your friends, your brothers and sisters, your dad, whoever it may be. That's what it's all about.'

Meyler got to the Premier League in an unorthodox way. Johnny Fallon, former Ireland kitman with an eye for a player, recommended that Roy Keane take a closer look at the kid who had just broken into the Cork City team. Keane was Sunderland manager at the time and didn't wait around. He got the club to make a formal offer to Cork, which was accepted, and Meyler boarded the next flight with his father to sign the contract.

It took a little time for him to break into the first-team set-up, and then he suffered a cruciate knee ligament injury that derailed his momentum. Injuries became an unfortunate hallmark of his career, first at Sunderland and then at Hull City.

'I get asked all of the time to speak to men and women, boys and girls, who go through a cruciate ligament knee injury. Sometimes I say yes, sometimes I say no,' shares Meyler. 'I can sit down and talk to you about what it's going to be like from the moment you arrive into surgery. I can tell you what you're going to feel like when you wake up. I can tell you what it's going to be like for the first six weeks when you struggle to sleep, to shower, you need help going to the toilet. I can talk you through all of that but the first thing you have got to overcome is that mental challenge. I won't say I struggle talking to people about it but [I want them to know that] I'm not you and you're not me.

'I remember the surgeon saying to me: "My concern is that you won't do everything I tell you to do in order to get back playing again." So I said: "My concern is that you don't botch the surgery." I love nothing more than someone who has confidence in their own ability and I had a guy called Steve Bolland, who was hugely confident. Even when I had trouble with my knee towards the end of my career, he was my first phone call. But the point is that Steve said that I had to do the work and that is what I have to tell other people – it's going to be tough. I've had seven surgeries across both knees throughout my career. I need a metal knee now because it still causes me pain. The injuries were tough.'

Of course, there were days when he couldn't see a light at the end of the tunnel, but consistency was his shield to hold off complacency. A daily routine of undergoing his rehab exercises from 7 a.m. to 10 a.m. allowed him time to watch the first-team squad train. The last thing he wanted was to be 'out of sight, out of mind', so he stayed around as much as possible. He travelled to away games, he stood in the corner of the changing room, he engaged with his team-mates without ever becoming a distraction. It was all part of his recovery.

While he did return to playing after the injuries, and enjoyed some of his most memorable moments during that period, he knew he was on the clock. Time was ticking down on how long his knees would hold up. Meyler got the most out of them and feels proud of what he achieved before he decided that enough was enough – finishing up at Coventry City in 2019 after a brief spell with Reading.

'When I retired I had a chat with Roy Keane and he said that I had a wonderful career. I'm thinking that he has won seven Premier League titles and one Champions League, he's inducted into the Hall of Fame, and, for me as a Corkman, I think he is the greatest-ever Irish player, so it was amazing to hear him say that to me. There are many variations of success. You don't have to do x, y and z to have a brilliant career. If I hadn't have played in the Premier League and I stayed with Cork City, I'd love to have achieved what someone like Paul Osam did in the League of Ireland.'

Again he brings it back to the almost surreal fact of having been a Premier League player. 'I think to get to play in the Premier League is an achievement in itself. You look at how few Irish lads are in the Premier League now. That's not a knock on them but just an example of how hard it is to get in. I was very fortunate to have played in the Premier League. So, yes, I do see my career as a success.'

Meyler jokes that he holds the most unwanted Premier League record: the only player to have been head-butted by an opposing manager. That is in reference to a confrontation with former Newcastle United manager Alan Pardew when Meyler was attempting to retrieve a ball on the sideline for Hull City. They clashed. Tempers flared, words were spat out and Pardew lowered his head towards Meyler in an incident that now belongs on Christmas specials that show the lighter side of the Premier League.

There are many other reasons why Meyler should be remembered for what he did during his Premier League days. He was a warrior, a player who made it difficult for his opponents and someone his team-mates could rely on. He relished the big battles against the big teams and the framed jerseys that hang on the wall of his games room serve as a reminder of the star players he competed against.

Now, if only someone could find a clip of him humming along to Liverpool's anthem!

20
Stephen Ward

Wolverhampton Wanderers (2009–12), Burnley (2014–19, 2016–19)

Games Played: 171

Goals Scored: 6

Assists Created: 5

Clean Sheets: 28

Yellow Cards: 16

Red Cards: 1

Wins: 51

Draws: 40

Losses: 80

The glitz, the glamour and the Panini stickers. Stephen Ward remains grateful for everything that being a Premier League footballer brought him, but there was one particular day when it struck him just how lucky he was to have played in the most popular league in the world.

'One of the best feelings I've had off the pitch is when I brought my son, Jackson, to the shop when he was around six or seven years old, and I got him a packet of stickers and I was in it. His face and his reaction was great to see. It was mind-blowing to share that experience with him,' said Ward. 'He has walked out with me as a mascot for games, which was fantastic. I walked him out against Arsenal and against Chelsea and he's walking down the line shaking hands with all of these star players. But to be one of those players that he collected with his sticker albums felt quite special. His old man in there amongst the Premier League stars.'

Ward can recall his own experience of growing up in the Dublin suburb of Portmarnock and rushing to the local shop to tear open a packet of Merlin Premiership stickers (Panini would later take over from Merlin). The rebrand of England's top flight and its global ascent would come a number of years later, but that excitement of discovering which star player was in your packet had gripped Ward two decades before his son would share a similar feeling.

Not that Ward would ever describe himself as a star player. He is far too humble for that. And his journey to becoming a Premier League player is one weighted in pragmatism after trials with English clubs as a teenager led to his parents reminding him that education came first. In fact, it looked like he had missed the opportunity to earn a move to professional football when he joined Bohemians' Under-21 side in the League of Ireland once his Leaving Cert had been secured.

At that time, he was a gangly forward who was not exactly prolific in front of goal. Sure, he was involved with the Republic of Ireland Under-21s, but he needed a bit of luck to fall his way. Eventually that happened, with Wolverhampton Wanderers manager Mick McCarthy seeing the potential in Ward and taking a gamble on signing him in 2007 for a reported fee of £100,000.

Wolves were in the Championship at that time. It was the beginning of a career in English football, even if playing in places like Plymouth, Barnsley, Southend and Colchester was not what Ward had in mind. None of the opponents he would be facing each week were recognisable from his Panini stickers. This was an entirely different world, one where skill and technique was replaced with grit and determination.

For Ward, however, this was the chance that he had been hoping for. He was ready to roll his sleeves up and follow his team-mates into battle every week. McCarthy liked that about him and gave the then twenty-one-year-old game-time as a result. He would score three goals in his first season, but it was clear that he was not the goalscoring messiah that the Wolves fans were expecting to see lead their line.

He was fully aware of his own limitations. The son of astute parents – his father Sean was a well-respected member of An Garda Síochána for many years – Ward has never been afraid to tackle difficult moments in his life. He embraces challenges that fall his way and would be the ideal team-mate to have on a run through the *Crystal Maze* because he possesses the intellect to problem-solve and the selflessness to put others first. Perhaps these were the traits that McCarthy first identified in him, rather than merely focusing on what he could do with a football at his feet.

Ward's adaptability probably best explains why two-time Ireland manager McCarthy saw him as the ideal candidate to fill the void in their starting line-up when the regular left-back for Wolves was ruled out with injury. There was still time in the transfer window to draft in a replacement, but McCarthy felt something in his gut about transforming Ward from a forward into a defender.

Ward explains it best himself. 'In my second season I started to play wide on the left quite a bit and then the lad who was playing full-back did his cruciate [knee ligament]. Mick pulled me into his office and said that I could do a job there and that he wasn't going to bring anyone in as a replacement. He said that he could mould me into a left-back with how I was as a player. We went on to win the league [Championship] that year and get promoted, so I never looked back on it.

'I always felt as a striker that I could score goals and had that attacking instinct, but when I first arrived in England I could see the difference in what you needed to make it as a striker. But we all know that strikers are notorious for being self-centred on the pitch and it's their job to score goals.

I was a little bit different as a striker as I would close down from the front, I would do a lot of donkey work running the channels and winning fouls, so my better games were when I probably didn't score. I realised when I arrived in England that there was an expectancy on the striker to hit double figures. I based my game around a lot of other things. If I'm being honest I don't think I would've had the career I've had if I stayed as a centre forward. I wasn't prolific enough at that level. But the timing helped me because around the time that I switched to left-back there was a big focus on full-backs having that dual threat and being able to attack. I had the part going forward, but it was about learning how to defend.'

If he wasn't before, Ward became a student of the game. He would laser his focus in on the performance of left-backs, noting their body shape, the timing of their interceptions, their positioning off the ball, their angles in holding a defensive line and how they overlapped or underlapped when breaking forward on runs. Whether it was *Match of the Day*, a live game on Sky Sports or extra footage from the club's Performance Analysis Department, Ward soaked up as much information as he could. This was the equivalent of a striker staying behind after training to engage in extra shooting practice.

It paid off too as Ward established himself as the regular left-back for club and country. Having earned promotion with Wolves to the Premier League in 2009, he then got the first of his fifty senior international caps in 2011 in the Carling Nations Cup – scoring in a 5-0 victory over Northern Ireland. Within a year he would be lining out in the UEFA European Championships in Poland.

Everything was starting to work out. Ward was still learning the new position but he looked comfortable there and people quickly forgot that he was previously a striker. And he didn't look out of place among other Premier League left-backs at the time, such as Ashley Cole, Patrice Evra and Gaël Clichy. Sure, they were more clinical and polished, but the Dubliner very much belonged in the full-back union.

Then, a bolt of irony struck in December 2010, when Ward enjoyed one of his finest performances in the Premier League – as a centre forward. For one night only, he was asked to switch back to his old position for a trip to Anfield to take on Liverpool.

'We had a striking crisis,' explained Ward, who can hardly hide the smile on his face as he recalls the type of night of which all kids aspiring to become footballers dream. 'Mick [McCarthy] liked to play 4-4-2 so that we had a chance of retaining the ball when we cleared it. Steven Fletcher was just back from injury and Kevin Doyle was out. I remember Mick pulled me [aside] in the hotel before the game and said that he was going to play me up front alongside Sylvan Ebanks-Blake. I hadn't played there in quite a while, but I was willing to give it a go. I was more there to cause a bit of carnage, get after them and play slightly deeper so I could almost be an extra body in midfield. And then I scored the winning goal and we won 1-0!

'I was a Man United fan growing up and, funnily enough, my mum's side of the family are all Liverpool, so they had split loyalties that day. Weirdly, I've had a lot of Liverpool fans come up to me when on holidays and shake my hand for scoring that goal because Roy Hodgson was their manager at the time and I think he got sacked a week later so they got a new manager out of it. It's a goal that I'll never forget.'

Typically, the euphoria of scoring that goal is guarded closely. Occasionally, however, it is pushed forward to his mind's eye and replayed like an old cinema reel. Not that you will ever catch Ward boasting about such a feat. In fact, he spent the majority of his Premier League career fearing that it could end at any moment. He had three seasons in the top flight with Wolves before suffering relegation in 2012. A move to Burnley brought him back for four more seasons, yet he never felt secure throughout that time.

There wasn't a moment when he allowed himself to relax in the knowledge that he had fulfilled a childhood dream of reaching the Premier

League. He had to keep fighting to keep it alive. So when others around him were doubling, and sometimes tripling, their annual salaries, he chose to focus on building up minutes on the pitch rather than bulking up his bank account.

Should he have stuck his neck out and demanded a little more? Could he have earned significantly more than he did? It's something that Ward has thought about but it's not an issue that will keep him awake at night. The thing that mattered most was the football, not the money.

'When I came to Wolves it was about mapping out a career for myself. I speak to a lot of young lads now who say "Oh, he played in the Premier League, he must have been this or that. But I have lived football through two different eras. The first era was when the Premier League wages probably weren't even as good as the Championship wages because the TV money only came in around 2011, 2012 or 2013 [i.e. when the international TV rights hit record heights]. When I went to Burnley, even though they were not big payers compared to other clubs, it [the salary] was bigger than what I was previously on. For me, it wasn't about asking for more … I've always had that mentality of having to prove myself. Maybe sometimes I undervalued myself or didn't realise how well I was doing at times. If a club was coming to me offering me a new deal I had more satisfaction in knowing that I was doing something right at the club.

'Regardless of what they were offering me, as long as it was better than what I was on and it was a longer term, I was pretty much happy to sign it. Maybe that cost me a few quid throughout my career. But when I was at Wolves, there wasn't the enormous sums that they talk about now in the Premier League, and then when I went up with Burnley I felt that I had to prove myself again.'

And he feels that he did prove himself during that second stint in the Premier League. 'It was only then that I felt like a Premier League player, those next four years. I felt like I deserved to be there. Not that I deserved X amount of money but that I deserved to be in the Premier League and I was more comfortable there at that time compared to when I was previously there with Wolves.'

It's safe to say now that Ward did enough to justify his position as a Premier League footballer. In terms of Irishmen to feature the most in the league, he is thirty-third overall on 171 appearances. Not a bad return for a kid from Portmarnock who started out as a striker and transformed himself into a left-back known for his consistency.

Having played in the League of Ireland and in every professional tier in England (his later years saw him line out for Ipswich Town in League One and for Walsall in League Two), Ward has the scars to prove that he has been through more than a few demanding contests in his career.

International football was a different kind of level and he excelled there too – particularly during Martin O'Neill's reign, when he helped Ireland reach the last sixteen of Euro 2016 – but the Premier League is where he was tested most often.

Even if it was not in the way most people would think. 'People talk about how gruelling the Championship is, where it is a game every Saturday then another on a Tuesday. In the Premier League, the physicality and the pace is there in every game. But the thing that is different in the Premier League compared to any other league is the mental side. You are mentally drained after every game,' he said. 'You cannot switch off for one second during a Premier League game because if you do you get punished, and that's the reality of it. There is so much focus on every game that it's a blessing when you don't play in the mid-week [fixture] because it's very difficult to recover. Physically, you become accustomed to it because you are training at that level and your body gets used to the intensity of the games, but mentally it can be very draining, especially if you were in a relegation battle.

'Unless you were part of a top-ten team then you were always looking over your shoulder. You look at the fixture list and your next four games are Man United, Chelsea, Liverpool and Man City, and you're thinking:

"Where the hell are we going to get a point from?" So mentally I think it is a lot more demanding than any of the other leagues.'

Again, it comes back to a sense of belonging at that level. 'There is a fear factor that comes with playing in the Premier League. You're playing Man City away and you're thinking: "I don't want to come off here looking like I don't belong in this league." So all of that mental energy that you use to prepare for games is physically demanding as well, if that makes sense? People say it's the hardest league in the world and it is.'

Ward can ease up now in the knowledge that he made it to the 'hardest league in the world' and thrived there. He most definitely belongs in that packet of stickers among the other Premier League stars.

21

Jonathan Walters

Bolton Wanderers (2002–03), Stoke City (2010–17), Burnley (2017–18)

Games Played: 233

Goals Scored: 43

Assists Created: 19

Clean Sheets: 41

Yellow Cards: 26

Red Cards: 1

Wins: 77

Draws: 65

Losses: 91

The career of a professional footballer is often compared to a rollercoaster ride with adrenaline-filled highs followed quickly by soul-searching lows. Jonathan Walters certainly knows how that feels, having started out in the Premier League, before dropping three levels down to League Two, and rising back up again to the top.

Walters, therefore, is someone who can accurately provide an insight into life as a Premier League player. And in many ways, that perspective can be broken down into three stages: The Good, The Bad and The Ugly.

The good

Nothing beats that first appearance. For a footballer to make their senior debut, it is a stamp of approval that indicates that they have made it. Walters got that with Bolton Wanderers in the 2002–03 season when appearing as a substitute in a 2-1 loss to Charlton Athletic. He went on to feature in four Premier League games for Bolton before his career took another direction. Those four games were not enough to establish himself in that league but they did present him with the opportunity of making his grandmother proud as she got to see him play at the highest level in England. That meant a lot to Walters, particularly since his Dublin-born mother had passed away when he was just a boy.

The journey to that point is an interesting one as Walters, who grew up in Merseyside, started out with Blackburn Rovers. 'I was at Blackburn as a youth and I was actually top scorer in England for my age. We got to the Youth Cup Final in my first year and I scored. I think I scored thirty-eight goals that year and I had never been in an academy before. Then I left and immediately went into the first-team squad with Bolton and was pretty much on the bench every week. I was given squad number 12 and I was like "bloody hell", I was immediately thrust into that side of it. It was mental because the team that they had was full of great guys like Colin Hendry, Per Frandsen, Henrik Pedersen, Kevin Nolan and Jussi Jääskeläinen. Then you had Youri Djorkaeff who had just won the World Cup [in 1998 with France].

'I was still a kid and I don't think I grasped it as much as I should have. It goes back to home life because I didn't have much of a home life. I wasn't living right … not in a bad way, I just spent as much time away from home as possible. I went on loan to a few clubs and I had two years left on my contract at Bolton but I asked to go to Hull because I had that taste of playing every week. Now I look back and think: what was I doing? Stay as long as you can at a Premier League club. I don't have any regrets because my career turned out how it turned out. But maybe it would have been slightly different if I had stayed at Bolton. It was a massive eye-opener there because Sam Allardyce was so far ahead of what coaches were doing at that time. It was an unbelievable experience for me to be around that.'

Even though he made his Premier League debut with Bolton, the most significant thing that he experienced at the club was the good habits that the senior professionals exhibited. Djorkaeff, in particular, caught Walters' attention by bringing simplicity to his shooting routine after training every day. There was nothing fancy about it; the France international just focused on hitting the target, again and again.

It didn't happen straight away, but Walters learned over time that it was the simple things that led to success. He discovered that maintaining a disciplined lifestyle, following a healthy diet and working as hard as possible in every session was the best way to enjoy consistency as a footballer. It is what helped him return to the Premier League six years after leaving Bolton in 2004.

The period that Walters spent in the lower leagues was full of uncertainty and off-field issues, but he did enjoy some good times, played a lot of games and discovered a hunger to be the best version of himself. 'People always ask: "Did you know that you were always going to get back there?" I always believed in myself but my focus was always on the team that I was in. I had a young family at the time so your focus is more on a week-by-week basis rather than on long-term targets.'

Following pit stops at Hull City, Wrexham, Chester City and Ipswich Town, he eventually did get back to the Premier League when he joined Stoke City in 2010. In his first season there, he finished as the club's joint-top goalscorer and proved that he belonged at that level. He would go on to play over 200 times for the Potters and establish a rapport with the supporters, who still view him as one of their best players of the Premier League era.

He immediately noticed the rise in standard once he was back in the top flight. 'Whatever league you go into you have to adapt but I was surprised when I got back to the Premier League, when I signed for Stoke, of the physicality of every player. Every player was six foot plus. Every player was quick. Every player was good with their feet. You watch the telly and think that a Premier League player is slow but there is no slow player in the Premier League – every player is quick.'

Good discipline became his way of competing at this level. 'I would go into the training ground for 6.30 every morning and go into the gym for an hour and a half. Everyone would be laughing because I was always in the gym, I wouldn't miss a day. I wasn't doing weights but stretching and core strength, whatever I needed to work on. After training I'd be back in the gym. I'd be eating right, living right and that's how I carried on throughout my career. I think I just saw in myself that I needed that discipline. Andy Wilkinson, who was there at Stoke at the time, had a brain injury and he had to retire because of it. I remember him telling me things about the brain. He said that a brain is like a computer because they had reset a part of his brain. So I bought a book about it and in the book it says that you don't properly start maturing until in your mid-twenties. I've seen that in a lot of players. But, for me, playing in the Premier League was all for my family; my wife, my daughters and my son. I wanted to make them proud and set them up for life. That was my work ethic in the Premier League and I was the fittest player in the league; I knew I was and my stats show that.'

It was during his time at Stoke that Walters became a regular starter for the Republic of Ireland, scoring fourteen goals in fifty-four appearances, playing in two UEFA European Championships and picking up the FAI Senior International Player of the Year Award in 2015.

There was also the FA Cup run in 2011 that brought Walters and Stoke all the way to the final at Wembley. They narrowly lost 1-0 to Manchester City but the statement was made that Stoke had the ability to mix it with the Premier League's top teams. They proved to be a nightmare opponent for Arsenal for many years, while there were also a couple of notable victories over Liverpool.

Walters was the team's most consistent performer for at least six of his seven seasons at the club. During that period he set a new club record of sixty-one consecutive appearances in the Premier League. The £2.75million that Stoke paid Ipswich for him was clearly money well spent.

Money became a by-product of thriving in the Premier League. The better he did, the more handsomely Walters was rewarded. Or at least that is how people on the outside would imagine it to be. In reality, he was nowhere near any of the top earners in the league despite being his team's best player for several seasons. He did make good money relative to the average national salary in the UK, of course, and he used as much of it as possible to cater for his family, pay off a mortgage and put some savings away. Time spent toiling away in the lower leagues will teach a player to be appreciative of their money. 'People often judge a player by what they won in their career. If you need trophies and winners' medals to tell you that you're a success it's not quite right. I understand that you want to be at the highest level but to get into the Premier League, to help set up my family and to help a lot of people less fortunate than myself, I've made a success of myself.'

All of that combined to make the good times particularly memorable, as the Premier League brought fame and fortune – even if they were on a modest level – as well as the opportunity to play in the 'best league in the world'.

The bad

Sometimes the bad isn't that bad at all. Take the Chelsea game on 12 January 2013 as an example. It should be marked down as Walters's worst-ever game as he scored two own goals and missed a penalty in a 4-0 defeat. It was a whole new level of embarrassment.

Except the aftermath of that game made him think twice about what constituted being a truly bad experience. 'First of all, I've scored the own goal. I think I've ran past three people to get the header in, it was a good diving header actually! Then I kicked the ball at my own face, scored another own goal and missed a penalty. I can either sulk about it and be down about it or you can realise that it's not that big of a thing when you think about some of the really bad things that happen in life. I remember going home and the kids taking the mick out of me, putting it on telly and laughing. We just laughed it off.'

Before he got home, Walters apologised to his team-mates in the changing room directly after the game and the manager, Tony Pulis, summoned him to a meeting the next day. The burly forward expected the worst from his manager and he did volley some verbal abuse in his direction but it was more playful than venomous. Walters was relieved, at least until Pulis informed him that he had to do an interview about the game. The last thing that he wanted to do was talk about his error-ridden performance in the media, but there was a catch – the fee associated with the interview would be donated to the Donna Louise Children's Hospice. This was a way of turning a bad experience into something good.

Still, the suffering wasn't over just yet for Walters. Initially he was due to sit out the midweek Cup tie away to Crystal Palace but Pulis felt that it would be good for him to play, to get the bad vibes out of his system. The Palace fans were licking their lips in anticipation of seeing the Stoke striker so they could not so kindly remind him of his Chelsea nightmare. As he trotted onto the Selhurst Park pitch he was greeted to a chant of 'He scores when he wants.' Walters cracked a wry smile, appreciating the sense of humour. Then he went and scored twice to silence them.

If positives can be taken from performances – no matter how bad they are – then the really bad side to the Premier League shows up in how brutal it can be as a business. Players are often seen as pawns, readily sacrificed when clubs are making bigger moves. 'As you start to play in the Premier League you come to the realisation that the club is looking to replace you. No matter you who are, what position you play or how well you're doing, the club is always planning to replace you. I was very conscious of that and it's why I played right wing, left wing, in the Number 10 [position], up front and even in midfield because I was willing to do the work that others wouldn't do.

'I remember one year I scored a silly amount of goals and I had a year left on my contract and asked my agent about it. And they said: "Yeah, we're not going to look at that now." So I carried on but a few months later we got around to negotiating. I wasn't asking for the top wage because I knew that the club were bringing in some very good players on very high wages. But it dragged on and then it looked like I might have to leave the club but I didn't want to go. In the end it got sorted and I signed a new deal, but I remember Tony Scholes [chief executive and director of the club at the time] – who is a great guy – saying to me that it was just business, it was never personal.'

No young player ever views the Premier League as a business that will eventually discard them. They see it as a land of opportunity, a footballing Oz where the yellow brick road leads to a lifetime of riches and glory. Sadly, however, there is always a man behind the curtain spinning propaganda to make them believe that the bad side doesn't exist. But it does.

The ugly

Walters is a family man. He spent his playing career living a quiet life away from the pitch. Part of that was due to his daughter Scarlett being born with gastroschisis – a birth defect in which the baby's intestines extend outside the abdomen – so that required a lot of hospital visits and close attention during her early years.

The other part was that Walters was aware of his status if he went for a night out. He was known to be an Everton fan, so Liverpool was off limits because there was 'always someone who would have something to say'. So he avoided that potential conflict altogether by staying home with his family. He knew that things could turn ugly very quickly just because he was a footballer that people could easily identify.

An uglier side to the Premier League, however, was in how players could be treated like machines: perform to the required level or else find yourself on the scrap heap. A bad side was when players were let down with contracts or by being moved on, but it got really ugly when they were dismissed altogether.

Walters feels that players do not receive the kind of support that they require – both during their careers and after it. It is why he applied to become CEO of the Professional Footballers' Association (PFA) in 2021. As a player he served on the PFA Management Committee and regularly voiced his concerns about the need to provide a better support structure for players. He believed that, as CEO, he could have implemented the kind of changes that the association and players throughout the football league in England needed.

'There are so many lows in football and you're lonely a lot. Trust is a big issue in football. You are close to your team-mates but there is such a turnover that it's hard to stay close to everyone. I think players have trust issues because a lot of people outside of football will try to take advantage of you, especially financially, and they will see you in a certain light. It's ridiculous the amount of players who've gone bankrupt and get divorced, so there is an issue there that needs addressing. One of the reasons why I went for the PFA role was that I want to help people and help players. I don't think the help is good enough, I really, really don't.

'You can see why so many people go through so many issues, because you're part of something for twenty years and suddenly you're not. No matter how much money you've got, you can quickly go through your money. You're quickly forgotten about by the players you played with, by clubs, by managers, etcetera. There is no after-care for footballers. I look at how they do it in rugby, in particular Harlequins, and how they help set up individuals for the rest of their lives and provide a support group.' This, Walters feels, is the way it should be done in football.

Every year there are hundreds of players who make up squad lists in the Premier League. They each share the ambition of succeeding in a competitive league, but the reality is that many will fall away. That is when the individual realises that being part of a team was always going to be a short-term thing and that fending for themselves should've been their priority from the very beginning.

The impact of being dumped by a Premier League club can be detrimental for a young man. It can lead to a loss of self-confidence, a hatred of the sport that they loved for so long, a tension in relationships that can lead to divorce and a mistrust of people – even those keen to help. This is the ugly side of the Premier League.

Walters has been through the good, the bad and the ugly. Yet he prefers to focus on the positive things that the Premier League has given him. And that is why he will continue to fight for better standards for players, so they too can experience the things that have transformed his life.

22

Paddy McCarthy

Crystal Palace (2014)

Games Played: 1

Goals Scored: 0

Assists Created: 0

Clean Sheets: 0

Yellow Cards: 0

Red Cards: 0

Wins: 1

Draws: 0

Losses: 0

'Ah, you only played one game in the Premier League.' Or: 'Wow, you got to play in the Premier League.' Paddy McCarthy has heard it all before. The different perspectives, the flimsy opinions, the clunky analysis. He doesn't particularly care for what others think of his Premier League experience; what matters is that he experienced it.

McCarthy is the type of person whose personality and ambition lures people in. He has always set high standards, for himself and for those around him. So it's hardly surprising that playing in the Premier

League was his aim from when he first fell in love with football. Yet, for much of his career he was the last romantic left rejected on the dancefloor every time he thought his flirtations with the Premier League were going to lead to a breakthrough. It happened with Manchester City, with Leicester and Charlton Athletic. And even when he did ultimately achieve promotion with Crystal Palace, injury sidelined him at the most important time.

Palace had just beaten Watford in the Championship play-off final in 2013. McCarthy could hardly wait to get started in pre-season. The Premier League was waiting. A training camp in Marbella, Spain had his competitive juices flowing. Then he felt a sharp pain in his groin area and that was when the worst period of his life took over.

A tough centre-back, McCarthy had an ability to read danger quickly. He was strong in the air. He was superb at getting out in front of his opponent to intercept passes. He was fluid with his passing and confident in his decision-making. He was vocal and the kind of leader that any goalkeeper would want in front of them and a midfield would want behind them. And just when he should have been bringing all of those qualities into the Premier League, he was diagnosed with osteitis pubis – chronic inflammation of the pubic area and surrounding soft tissues.

Every warrior has a moment when they get exposed as being a mere mortal; this was McCarthy's moment. Naturally, he tried to battle through it by taking injections and playing games feeling severe pain. But his body gave out on him and there was nothing he could do. 'In pre-season I had a really bad reaction to an injection into my pubic bone. I was playing through injury for a number of months and getting cortisone injections. I was captain, I was in good form and I was taking these injections to manage myself rather than take a period off to try and let it settle down. Then I had that bad reaction and it had a real adverse effect on me. I was twenty-seven, twenty-eight and I missed eighteen months of football through it.

'It was a tough time. I was going to specialists all over the world and they couldn't pinpoint what was wrong. They all agreed that it was a very serious thing that caused this massive amount of swelling all through my body, from my knees up to my chest. One surgeon described it like I was lit up like a Christmas tree. I couldn't walk for a large number of months, I couldn't pick my kids up, I couldn't kick a football with them. "Will I ever play again?" That was the sort of thing going through my head because all of the top guys couldn't give me any answers. It was tougher to take because I was in my prime years, so it was a bitter pill to swallow.'

McCarthy was desperate to return to what he loved: playing football, preferably in the Premier League. 'The club did try to send me to a psychologist but nobody could tell me anything that could help me. What would help me was getting back on a football pitch. So when I was going to see people, I didn't really want to listen at that time. I was in a bad place. I was sick of people asking me when would I be back. I was sick of going to see surgeons. I was sick of going into the gym but I was doing it because I was trying everything. I was grateful to have a great family around me, and friends too, but the only thing that would help me was getting back on a football pitch.

'Over months the swelling came down and then I got off crutches and was able to walk by myself. Then slowly but surely I was able to do exercises. I had a couple of operations on my groin and just built myself up. It was always touch and go whether I could get back to playing again. I remember going to the Germany national team doctor, Hans-Wilhelm Müller-Wohlfahrt, and had something like fifty injections, my eyes were spinning.'

When the return to playing came, it was unexpected. 'I'd play a couple of pre-season games and break down or play a reserve game and pull a quad or a calf or an Achilles. I never felt that I was going to be fit again and then one day Tony Pulis threw me in. We played against Wigan in the FA Cup and he just flung me in. I got through that game, which was on the Saturday, and I was still in pain on the Monday … every muscle in my body was all over the place. That was the first game back in eighteen months and I remember thinking that that was an achievement in itself just to get back on the football pitch. Then on that Tuesday night, I came off the bench against Hull to make that single appearance in the Premier League. But deep down I knew that my body wouldn't allow me to do the things that I could do a couple of years before. And I never was the same player. Slowly but surely it came away from me with injury after injury.'

McCarthy had a professional career for thirteen years yet his story is often – perhaps unfairly – characterised solely by the twenty-six minutes that he played on 28 January 2014. Introduced as a substitute for Yannick Bolasie in a 1-0 victory over Hull City at Selhurst Park, he had finally made it to the Premier League. 'I wouldn't have taken any satisfaction out of it if I had been fit throughout my career but it felt like an achievement because of what I had been through from that injury.'

To support that sentiment it's important to rewind back to when McCarthy left Belvedere to join Manchester City in 2000. Upon arrival at his new surroundings, he heard a familiar accent every day as the club had been busy recruiting some of the best Irish teenagers at that time. There was goalkeeper Brian Murphy, defender Stephen Paisley, midfielders Glenn Whelan and Willo Flood and striker Stephen Elliott. This band of Irish City Slickers instantly bonded, as they shared the common goal of making it in the Premier League.

'It was a dream to play in the Premier League, that was always the dream to get to the highest level. But I think most of us just wanted to play professional football and we felt that Man City at the time was the best place for us to develop as young men and a pathway into the first team. We saw it as a really big club, a sleeping giant, that felt right for us. We didn't really know each other until we went to Man City. I think the club identified players from Ireland who they believed had the right ability but more so the character to go on and have careers in the game. And that was proven definitely.'

McCarthy lived in the same house as Murphy and Alan Reilly, who was a few years older but also hailed from Ireland. In another digs – which are essentially local family homes who take in academy players from clubs every year – were Flood, Whelan and Elliott. They would meet up every day, train every day and socialise with each other every day.

Then things started to change as the reality of forging individual careers came into view. Murphy was the first to train with the first team, while McCarthy skipped ahead of them all when he started to play first-team games – albeit on loan with Boston United. At that stage, McCarthy and Murphy had moved into an apartment together. In the heart of Manchester, they became men. They washed and ironed their own clothes, they paid bills, they looked after their own gear and they even learned how to cook … well, it took a while to move away from pasta sauce plopped on top of plain pasta.

What was most important was making strides on the pitch. McCarthy was still only eighteen years old but he was determined to be seen as a first-team player, whether that was in a Man City jersey or not. 'Probably the defining moment for myself, I was in and around the squad, and then I went on a couple of loans to get a taste of first-team football. I went to Boston in League Two and had a reasonably successful loan spell there. It gave me a taste for playing at three o'clock on a Saturday and in front of fans and [seeing] what real pressure was like. Then I went in that same season to Notts County in a league above and, again, that was a great experience. I thought that this is what I want, I don't want to go back and play in the reserves.

'We had all got to the stage where we felt that we were ready to get in a first team somewhere. For me, at that time, I could see that there were four or five established international centre-halves ahead of me. When that one opportunity came for me, and I felt that I was ready after experiencing two successful loan spells, Kevin Keegan played Danny Mills at centre-half when he was a right-back. That was the moment that I thought that I wasn't going to get in there. That is when I knocked the door down and said: "I want to go and play first-team football and get my career under way."'

And that is exactly what he did. McCarthy left for Leicester City in March 2005, where he became club captain within eighteen months and could have been part of a promotion-winning team if financial troubles had not rocked the club. Then Charlton Athletic came in with an offer for him to be part of their promotion-chasing team.

'When I met Alan Pardew [then Charlton manager] in London, he presented to me the squad that he had and the players they were bringing in and [claimed] that they were going for promotion back to the Premier League. He sold me on a real good project. That move felt like it would give me a better chance to get to the Premier League rather than staying at Leicester. Everything was going well at Charlton, we were up there amongst a few other teams in the mix for promotion and then in January we sold Andy Reid to Sunderland and that had a massive effect on the whole squad and everything we did. We sort of plateaued and never seen out the season in the way we should have. That was an opportunity missed. I went there with the ambition to get promoted and we fell out of the play-offs towards the end. Then that summer Neil Warnock put in an offer to bring me from Charlton to Crystal Palace. They had just missed out in the play-off semi-final so I went to meet Neil Warnock and he sold me the project of Crystal Palace. They had an unbelievable squad and a manager who I felt was just right for me and would maximise my potential.'

McCarthy's relationship with Warnock proved to be a curious thing. Ultimately they worked well together and it's a reason why the eccentric manager, who oversaw over 1,000 games in English League football, trusted the Dubliner to be his captain.

'He [Warnock] had a way of managing everybody. He was such a master psychologist. I had an argument with our goalkeeper, Julian Speroni, at half-time in my first or second game. He had his goalkeeping gloves around my throat. I was giving out saying that Julian wasn't vocal enough in the game. And Neil Warnock comes in and says: "How have you started an argument with him? He hardly speaks to anybody." And I said: "That's exactly why I started the fucking argument." Neil would be quite clever in using his assistant, Mick Jones, to say things about you so that you heard them. He would be like "Any chance of Maccer winning a fucking header today?" He just knew when to give you an arm around the shoulder or a kick in the arse, and they were never too far apart.'

Unfortunately for McCarthy he hit another setback as Palace hit financial troubles – just like Leicester before – and Warnock moved on to Queens Park Rangers. In came a new board and George Burley as manager. He didn't last long, though, and Dougie Freedman took over. Everything appeared to be moving on up again before Freedman departed for Bolton Wanderers. The managerial merry-go-round had McCarthy's head in a spin. Ian Holloway then took over and Palace found the momentum required to get through the Championship play-offs and secure a seat at the top table of English football, aka the Premier League.

After years of set-backs, McCarthy had made it. But the cruelty of injury put his career on hold. So near, yet so far. Until, of course, he got to play in that single Premier League game.

There are no regrets or bitterness over how it panned out. McCarthy actually feels fortunate to count himself amongst the 197 Irishmen to have featured in the first three decades of the Premier League. But now it's a case of: what's next? He wants to keep looking forward.

Having stepped into the world of coaching, he has already enjoyed stints leading Palace's Under-16s and Under-18s. Now he is in charge of the Under-23s and has completed his UEFA Pro Licence. A jump into management is next on the agenda and anyone who has come across him can attest to the desire and skillset that should help him to be successful.

McCarthy jokes that it won't be his body that lets him down this time.

23
Kevin Doyle

Reading (2006–08), Wolverhampton Wanderers (2009–12), Crystal Palace (2013–14)

Games Played: 164

Goals Scored: 37

Assists Created: 15

Clean Sheets: 22

Yellow Cards: 11

Red Cards: 0

Wins: 43

Draws: 37

Losses: 84

Kevin Doyle, in his kitchen in Wexford, is using a large wooden spoon to stir the vegetables that are stewing in a pot. Dinner will be ready soon. Not that his nine-year-old son, Bennett, cares. He is too engrossed in his iPad, watching and re-watching highlights of Cristiano Ronaldo.

It wasn't that long ago that Doyle was playing against the Portuguese superstar. He scored thirty-seven Premier League goals across spells with Reading and Wolverhampton Wanderers. But Bennett doesn't care about that either. He is only interested in Ronaldo and Manchester United.

Doyle attempts to claw back some dignity. He takes the iPad from his son and searches for one of his goals. He hands the iPad back and looks at his son's face, hoping for a positive reaction, hoping for a moment where his past efforts are recognised and lauded by the boy who will carry on his legacy when he is long gone.

Finally, Bennett looks up and asks: 'Why are the pictures so grainy, Dad?'

Doyle turns back to stir the food again. He is no longer a Premier League goalscorer, he's just a dad making the dinner.

***

Pat Dolan has always had an eye for a player and the ability to convince anyone prepared to listen of their vast potential. Dolan is charming, funny and engaging. He could sell almost anything to anyone. But all he is interested in is helping players to reach the highest level. That is why he focused in on Doyle.

Upon first meeting Doyle, he stuck out his hand and pronounced that the Wexford native would go on to become a Republic of Ireland senior international. This wasn't some swindler trying to offload miracle hair grow, this was the St Patrick's Athletic manager who had more connections than Heuston Station. So Doyle listened, went to play for the Saints and then followed Dolan to Cork City.

Everything started to fall into place. Doyle broke into the Ireland Under-21 set-up and stood out in an extremely talented Cork City side as their top goalscorer. It was hardly surprising when English clubs began to take an interest. Reading, however, moved quickest, thanks to Dolan, whose late brother, Eamonn, was working at the club and convinced their chief scout to take a closer look.

Doyle says: 'On my radar was to try to get across to England. I was thinking about trying to get to the Championship and see what happens. I was never cocky enough, I suppose, to think that I would play in the

Premier League. I thought that I had enough ability but I never thought that far ahead, it was always baby steps.

England was something of a blank slate to Doyle. 'I'd never been on a trial so I didn't know what to expect. All I heard was different stories from lads coming back from England and they made it sound like it was an alien world and the toughest thing you would ever do. Personally I didn't find it that way as I went over and I was straight into it. I was lucky maybe, with the club, that Reading had good facilities, good manager, good people, so I felt at home straight away.'

The move also proved to be good timing. 'I was up to speed when I went over as I was halfway through a season in the League of Ireland while the rest of the lads were only starting pre-season. So fitness-wise I was right up there and I started well with a couple of goals in pre-season games, so I went from being signed as a back-up striker to someone who the club thought could start games if needed.

'A lucky coincidence is that in the season that I signed Reading went on to have the best season ever in the Championship. You need a lot of luck but you also need to be ready to take your luck when it comes. I was the most confident that I would have been. I was leaving the League of Ireland with Cork City top of the league, we had just come off a good European run the year before, I was top scorer, I was in the Ireland Under-21 team, so I was going to Reading at a really good stage.'

Doyle was no ordinary League of Ireland export. In a way, he smashed through the glass ceiling because he went straight into a competitive Reading team pushing for promotion to the Premier League and Cork City received a decent transfer fee for him (as well as Shane Long, who was part of the package).

In previous years, many players left the League of Ireland for England only to return soured by the experience. Doyle believes his grounding at Cork helped to ensure that wasn't the case for him. He had become accustomed to thriving in a demanding environment and competing for his place among many of the league's finest players.

'Playing for Cork City at the time ... we had full houses, the coverage and press was massive. Actually I think the press coverage really prepared me for how to deal with it in England. When you are playing for Cork, there is no way that you can be anonymous. You are a professional footballer and there was pressure to perform. Two years there got me used to that side of football. It would have been a big leap if I hadn't have had that experience of European games and the pressure of playing for a big club like Cork City. Also [there were] some really excellent players at Cork City at that time ... Roy O'Donovan, John O'Flynn, George O'Callaghan, Liam Kearney, Neale Fenn, Alan Bennett, Joe Gamble, Dan Murray, Danny Murphy, Neal Horgan, Mick Devine, Billy Woods, Denis Behan, and Colin O'Brien was just finishing up. All-round quality.'

Upon arriving at Reading, Doyle had to prove that he belonged. 'I felt pressure to stay over in England. I think I signed a two-year contract and I remember in my head going, "don't let it be just the two years". So many people go and come back and it doesn't last. After I went over, it seemed like a lot more players went over and had longer careers in England. Before I went, there hadn't been anyone in ages, it seemed like. That was my fear, my worry, what drove me, how do I get past this initial two years.'

He recalls how he was something of a mystery to his new team-mates: 'I did get the feeling in the first week or two that the lads in England would've known nothing about me. I might as well have been coming from a pub league as they knew nothing about the League of Ireland. Just like any job that you join, your colleagues judge you when you first come in. But once I was able to show that I was up to speed in training and I scored in a couple of those pre-season games it was never really mentioned again.'

Doyle would go on to score eighteen goals in his first season with the Royals as they clinched promotion to the Premier League in 2006. His goalscoring form continued in England's top division the following season, with thirteen goals netted, as he was nominated for the PFA Young Player of the Year award (alongside Cesc Fabregas, Wayne Rooney, Micah Richards and Cristiano Ronaldo). Life, it seemed, was on fast forward.

It was around that time, however, that tactical changes started to have an impact on his game. Doyle describes it as the 'dying art of a centre forward' as teams largely ditched having two strikers up front to just one, or sometimes none. The role of the frontman was no longer about scoring goals but pressing defenders, creating space, holding up play, linking with team-mates on advancing runs and, generally, being used as a battering ram.

Doyle says that his own game needed to be tweaked after he tore a hamstring in his third season at Reading. All of a sudden he lost a yard of pace, so he stopped making runs in behind opposition backlines in order to come short and get involved in the play. It was either that or fill the role of battling for aerial balls to flick on for a fellow striker, which is what his international career with Ireland largely consisted of.

Still, he was a striker and strikers are expected to score goals. Fans don't care about the intricate details that a manager gives to their players, they see players in certain positions charged with certain duties. Doyle understood that but goalscoring became a lot tougher as his Premier League journey continued with a move from Reading to Wolves.

'As years went on, comparing my first few years at Reading to later on, it was so different. At Reading we had two out-and-out wingers in Glen Little and Bobby Convey who only wanted to cross the ball into the centre forward. We did all of the high-energy running and pressing but those lads just wanted to create assists, so there was constant service coming in. Actually [Cristiano] Ronaldo ruined it for centre forwards because all he cared about was scoring goals and all of the other wingers started copying him. Now wingers are expected to produce fifteen goals a season so they all cut in and have a shot. The game has changed. But definitely, as it went on, it became harder to score goals because the role of a centre forward changed.

'I suppose it depends on the club you're at and where you are, whether you are fighting relegation or if you're higher up the table. You don't have that luxury of having a striker hang around trying to score goals, they have to marry everything and do a lot more. I would've liked to score more goals, especially later in my career. Most of my goals came in the first part of my career, but I suppose my game changed in the second part. In my worst periods, I always went nine or ten games without scoring and then I managed to get one. If you went into double figures the press would be getting on to you then. But it's part and parcel of the job. As a striker you're treated better, you're paid better, so you have to take the other sides of it maybe more than what the midfielders or defenders get.'

Another perk of being a striker is the extra attention. At one point it was rumoured that Arsenal were admirers of Doyle and a move up to the table to join them was mooted. 'I was kept away from all of that, really. I tried to keep my head down and get on with things. I do remember a few different bids coming in for me and I was close to joining Aston Villa around then. I was only at Reading for a year and a half, I was getting used to living in England, I was happy so I didn't push for anything. Later on, a year or two later, different people were sniffing around but it didn't happen for whatever reason. I wasn't one to push it, I was happy to just be playing in the Premier League. Looking back, maybe if I had a few more years in England I might've looked at it differently. But I had a fabulous career, I did way better than most, so I don't look back and think if, but or maybe.'

One of the reasons why Doyle was able to make the most of his Premier League career was because he treated it like a job. Instead of saying that he had training the next day, he would describe it as 'work'. It was a deliberate attempt to disconnect from such a demanding industry that would leave him drained for days after each game – physically and mentally. Doyle tried to maximise the many idle hours that come with being a professional footballer. He would read books on long bus journeys, he would play golf just to get out in the fresh air and he even tried flying lessons. But football is all-consuming and it proved difficult to balance anything else with it, especially once he had kids to run after.

Doyle tries to simplify what being a Premier League player really means. He has been beneath the glossy veneer and insists that, in spite of its incredible global reach and commercial power, it remains simply a sport where twenty-two players compete for three points (or one).

'When you're looking at a big game on TV, you're thinking it's all so glamorous and so out of this world,' says Doyle. 'It's not. It's just lads going training, going back to sit in a hotel room waiting for the next meal or team meeting. When you think about it its a non-existence for a large part of your career ... you train, eat as healthily as you can and try to reserve your energy for a match. It's probably not natural but that's the way it is. It's weird because you're together with a bunch of fellas for eleven months of the year, pretty much every day – even Christmas Day. You mightn't like some of them yet you have to spend so much time with them on buses, in rooms and meetings. It's a strange one, but it's like that in most sports.'

Life as a Premier League footballer can feel like a goldfish bowl existence. Doyle certainly felt that while living in Birmingham, where it felt like there was an opinionated fan at every turn – broadcasting their allegiances to either Aston Villa, Birmingham City or Wolves. Even a pre-season trip to South Korea brought the kind of fanfare that one would expect to be reserved for pop stars, not a low-key striker with a mid-table Premier League team. It wasn't until he moved to the United States later in his career, to join Colorado Rapids in the MLS, that he found some sort of anonymity.

Now, he can enjoy the comfort of not being noticed. He coaches his son's Under-10s team and they don't care about his past. Their fathers do and they are the ones who request photos 'for their sons'. But, overall, Doyle can dip in and out of the world of football whenever he chooses. He does some TV work as a pundit then disappears back home to resume his role as a dad.

24

Seamus Coleman

Everton (2009 – Present)

Games Played: 329

Goals Scored: 21

Assists Created: 24

Clean Sheets: 89

Yellow Cards: 33

Red Cards: 2

Wins: 133

Draws: 93

Losses: 103

Honours: PFA Team of the Year

Time is a curious thing in the world of Seamus Coleman. He believes that being punctual is a virtue. He insists on sharing moments with fans until they have had their fill. He makes the most of every second walking across a hotel lobby, airport terminal or stadium car park to enthusiastically greet those whose eyes lock onto him. He wakes each morning with his mind drawing up plans for how he can maximise his day and give as much as he can to his club and country. He spends afternoons and evenings running after his children or checking in with them via FaceTime when work takes him on the road. Time is something that Coleman gives to everyone, yet it is the one thing that people tell him that he is running out of. Well, they don't exactly tell him but rather tweet it or write it or whisper it when he's not around. They say that his Premier League adventure is about to end. That makes him laugh because he was never meant to have made it to this level, never mind tough it out for thirteen successive seasons. So time is a commodity that he respects and never takes for granted.

Our conversation takes place in Castleknock Hotel during an afternoon off from the Republic of Ireland camp. Except Coleman has divided his 'time off' to cater for others. He does steal an hour for yoga in the morning before going for lunch with team-mates and then turning up for this interview. Everything is perfectly planned so that he has enough time to complete each task and then not be late for dinner when the squad reassembles. This is typical of the man, always respectful of the clock – or the digits on his iPhone.

There is so much to chat about with Coleman, who is arguably one of Ireland's most successful players of the Premier League era despite not picking up any winners' medals with Everton. The longevity alone is something to marvel at, especially when one takes into account that he missed a year with a serious leg injury, and that his club have tried and tested many competitors in his right-back position. He has seen them all off. Even in the twilight of his career he is still fighting with the same intensity as he did on the first day he arrived at the Everton training ground in January 2009, fresh from a surprise move from Sligo Rovers in the League of Ireland. His attitude to working hard has never changed.

Between the timekeeping, the work ethic, the passion and the fact that he is one hell of a footballer, Coleman makes the perfect captain. He insists that he would be the same whether or not he were in possession of a captain's armband. Yet his leadership qualities do stand out and were shaped by his upbringing in the small fishing town of Killybegs, County Donegal.

It's clear he doesn't take the role of captain lightly. 'I think when you have been somewhere for so long you feel things more, no matter if you are a captain or not. I don't want to sound like "Mr Everton" here but I don't just go home after training or a game and say "that's work done". It's everything you're thinking about. Obviously you spend time with your family and kids, but after that it's all you think about. Is the captaincy a burden? Or is it just that longevity and that love of the club? The people who you see around the club on a daily basis, you feel that pressure for them as well.

'I think [the nature of] captaincy and management has changed over the years. Before you might have been able to say how it is or rule with an iron fist but now it's maybe a case of putting your arm around the shoulder a bit more. It's changing what motivates a player, so you've got to know your team-mates and know how to manage them. There is a lot of one-to-one talks, especially when someone signs for the club, or text messages after a bad run of form, or text messages if a player ends up scoring after having a tough time, just always letting them know that you are there for them through the good and bad.

'For me, it's important when a player comes to the club that they are made to feel welcome. As a captain, I feel it's my responsibility for players to feel part of it all, to feel part of the club. Sometimes you have players with family on the other side of the world who they haven't seen in a long time and even though you can't do much for them, it's important for them to know that you are there for them.'

Surely, though, it is a challenge to connect with a player whose first language might not be English and for whom landing in Merseyside might feel like arriving on the dark side of the moon?

Coleman insists there is always a way to make a difference. It could be a friendly smile, a fist bump, an arm around the shoulder or even a simple text message that can be instantly translated via Google.

There are two sides to being a captain at a Premier League club. One is about protecting your team-mates, manager and club at all costs. The other is presenting a public image that reassures fans, sponsors, stakeholders and broadcasters that you, and your club, are doing the right things for the right reasons. It was the second part that Coleman had to deal with during the outbreak of COVID-19 in 2020, when the world shut down and Premier League clubs lost their composure. An over-reaction to the pandemic saw clubs place staff members on furlough – or cancel their contracts altogether – and ask players to take pay cuts. The slick, commercial machine that the Premier League markets itself as suddenly started to stutter, more like an old steam engine running short on coal.

In an effort to stabilise things, the captains from each of the twenty Premier League clubs got together – via online Zoom calls – to shape a strategy. Coleman was the sole Irishman involved.

'It was a stressful time for everyone because COVID was all very new for everyone and it was very worrying. Everyone was pressing the panic button, whether it was clubs, the Premier League or broadcasters. I remember being on Zoom calls for hours upon hours at the beginning. It was a massive thing to be part of and we made a big gesture for the NHS in the end [creating a charitable fund, called #PlayersTogether, which aimed to raise in excess of £4 million], which was great to be able to do. Everyone played their part on the calls and had something to say. As much as footballers get a bad reputation at times in the media, there are players who are really good people who really want to help the clubs and their communities.'

As captain, it is Coleman's job to set the standard on the pitch and the mood off it. When asked what traits he expects of each of his team-mates, it is hardly a coincidence that the first thing that he turns to is time-keeping. 'Be on time, be respectful, train hard, give it everything in every game, be appreciative of the staff and people around the club,' says Coleman. 'All of that, for me, will always go back to my parents … saying please, thank you, treating people right. I've carried that through my football career. You can respect people but you can call people out when they're not doing their job.'

Our conversation is interrupted. A hotel guest, who has circled around us twice to confirm that it is indeed the Ireland skipper sitting there in the foyer to the patio dining area, plucks up the courage to ask for a selfie.

Coleman is more than obliging, giving the stranger just the right amount of time to be courteous without it becoming awkward for either. You would think this sort of distraction would have become incredibly tiresome for Coleman after so many years, yet he greets every fan with the same level of enthusiasm, as if it were the first time he had been asked for a piece of his time. It is the sort of reaction we wish all professional athletes would give, but Coleman isn't like everyone else.

The way that he interacts with people goes some way to explain why he has remained loyal to Everton. In an era when players collect more clubs than points on their grocery shopping, it is bizarre that Coleman has actually been criticised for not looking to move away from a club that has treated him so well – and vice versa.

'To get to the level that I got to is not something I ever thought I would get to. When I was at St Catherine's in Donegal, that was my club. When I was at Sligo Rovers, that was my club. And when I moved on to Everton that became my club. I had a great manager at the time in David Moyes who ensured that you never got ahead of yourself, that you were earning your stripes every single day. I had that at Sligo with Paul Cook and it stuck with me. But I suppose it's just the person I am, that I work hard every day to get into the team and to stay in the team.

'Everton signed a lad from Sligo for £60,000 or whatever the fee ended up being, they gave me a chance without a trial and looked after me immensely when I was over there. I had gone to Celtic and Burnley on trial, but the longer that I was at Everton I really loved it and my family got settled there. So I wouldn't say it was a lack of ambition (about not moving on), I think it's more my personality that I was not going to be knocking on the chairman's door saying "you have to make this [move] happen". I never wanted to disrespect the football club by being that type of player who hands in a transfer request because I didn't get my way.

'I was brought up in a family that appreciates respect for others. For me, it would have been a kick in the teeth to a club that has been so good to me and is still so good to me. People can say that I could have moved on to whichever clubs were interested at the time, but I just didn't feel like I wanted to push that because I was happy where I was and I wanted to achieve things at the club.'

It's clear that his love for the club has not waned over the years. 'There's just something about Goodison Park on a Saturday that is special. The Everton in the Community side of things [EitC is one of the UK's top sporting charities; it is considered one of the Premier League's leading community schemes due to the quality and reach of its various programmes] is amazing and it's part of my personality in what I've always aspired to do: in looking after people in any way that I can. There was something about the club that gripped me from the beginning. But I'm not naive enough [not] to know that there will come a time when I will have to go, when I'm not good enough anymore and the club looks to bring someone in. But I never think that I should've went here or should've went there.'

It's not just that Coleman has been afforded plenty of game-time or enjoyed hearing the fans sing his name – his love for the club is far more deep-rooted. In March 2017, he suffered a horrific leg break while playing for Ireland against Wales and there were immediate fears that his career was in jeopardy. It was bad timing as the defender had been due to formalise a contract extension with Everton before that international window. The club, understandably, could have had second thoughts.

Coleman explains: 'I came away with Ireland and broke my leg. I was due to sign a contract in the week before I went away … I don't know why it didn't happen, I don't know why I didn't sign that week. Maybe I said I would do it when I came back or the chairman said to go away with Ireland and sign it when I came back. But I was about to sign a five-year contract, everything was agreed, and then I broke my leg. I think it was the second night I was in hospital when I got a phone call from the chairman saying: "Don't worry, son, get yourself right and that contract is still waiting for you here when you come back." Maybe I'm wrong but I don't think a lot of clubs would've had that response. I think they would've been in the background going "we've offered him this but let's take some off it and give [him] that". But nothing changed, the contract was sitting there waiting for me when I got back to the club a month later. Things like that I don't think you can forget.'

The topic switches from loyalty to motivation. Even someone of Coleman's boundless positivity must find it difficult to maintain a level of consistency when arrows of criticism get sharper and closer with each misplaced pass or crushing defeat. While he insists that he remains as committed as ever, it is quite another thing for team-mates who may be spoilt by handsome wages and lucrative bonuses.

'The one thing that I have not done in my thirteen years in football is give less than 100 per cent in every training session and every game. I think that is what you need across the board if you are to be successful. Some people arrive and maybe don't have that so they might need a push in the right direction. If they can find that love or that reason why they came into the game in the first place, because I do think along the way money and success can dampen that fire in the belly a little bit. So you have to make sure that lads don't lose that. For me, personally, I go out every single day to impress the team-mate beside me, the manager and the coaches. I still feel like that seventeen-year-old every single day.

'I suppose when you had to earn contracts to feed your family, or whatever the case may be, you couldn't sulk, you had to find a way to get into the team. Now, players across the board are on big contracts and whether they play or don't play they are getting paid regardless. Their ego might not want to let them show that they care so it's a bit of chest out bravado: the manager doesn't pick me [therefore] I don't like him or I don't like that. That's the side of it that you see that you don't like and it's not just at Everton, it's across the board in the Premier League … you see it with players falling out with managers all of the time. But if you had to fight to get into that starting eleven [in order to get a good salary], like it was in the early nineties, then it would be a different story.'

Another thing that has changed with time is the quality that the Premier League has ascended to. Tactically it has become more complex, technically it has become more advanced and physically it has become more draining. As a result, Coleman has to constantly adapt his own game. He does his homework on the iPad, watching clips of opponents, downloading the insights that the club's performance analyst provides, and asking the right questions in team meetings. Yet some of the learning has to happen in real time during a game, when, he insists, timing is everything – when to go forward, when to hold a position, when to intercept, when to check inside.

'When I first came into the Premier League, you might've been up against a left-footed left winger and that's what you're up against for the game. But now you go to somewhere like Man City away and, my God, you don't know whether you are coming or going. They have players in here, out there, left-backs coming inside, midfielders going wide. Everyone now is fast, fit and strong. Even players who are not the most talented in the Premier League are still a threat because of the physicality. It's a tough, tough league. It's a game for ninety minutes where you can't switch off. Shuffling as a backline, shuffling as a midfield just to close the gaps, but a team like Man City have so much quality that it's difficult to keep them out for the ninety minutes. But in saying that you wouldn't want it any other way, it's the league to be in. It's the best league in the world.'

As he approaches his mid-thirties, Coleman knows that his time playing at the top level is coming to an end. It's something that he does not fear but accepts. And already he is making plans for the future, having completed his UEFA A Licence as part of his coaching pathway.

Naturally, many people will assume that a good captain will morph into being a good manager. That isn't always the case. Besides, Coleman is blocking that type of thinking out of his mind; he still has a job to do on the pitch.

'You can go too much into it, thinking as a coach. I'm a player and I want to focus on what I have to do as a player. If you are sitting down to watch a game like Barcelona versus Real Madrid, you do look at the shape they are playing or the positions that certain players take up. They are things you wouldn't have thought about maybe five years ago, you would've just watched the game. As much as you want to take little bits from all of the managers you've worked with, and I do, you still have to remember what the end goal is and that is to do as well as I can as a player for my team.'

Again, we are interrupted and, again, Coleman rises to his feet with a bounce in his step. This time a grandfather wants to introduce his grandson to Coleman. The boy, probably nine or ten years old, is shy or perhaps a little overawed at meeting a Premier League footballer. Coleman has picked up a few tricks through the years, however, and engages with the boy as if they are lifelong friends. The grandfather beams in delight; he couldn't have picked a better role model to inspire the boy.

It is a mark of the man that he has not forgotten the boy he was. When he sees kids with a football under their arm or at their feet, he wants to treat them the same way he would have liked his footballing heroes to have been with him. Coleman appreciates that time can change a person, but it doesn't have to dilute their values, ambitions or manners.

'You have to remember where you are [from]. You have to remember being that little five- or six-year-old who spent hours and hours kicking the ball against the wall. Remembering the young lad playing for St Catherine's who gave everything that he possibly could. And the lad who went to Sligo and the manager who told him no but you never gave up. If you don't remember all of that it will be gone quick enough because it's a short career.

'There's good days and bad days, but you can't lose that fire in the belly because if you do then there's no point in kicking a ball any more. I can remember my dad finishing a night shift in the hotel, getting back in the car to drop me off for training at Sligo for the week but we found out after training that we were off the next day. So I rang Dad, who had just driven the hour and a half back home, to tell him I'm off. He came back for me, with a nudge from my mum to help ... she always played a big part in things, both of my parents did. You can't forget all of the sacrifices that other people have made for you to be where you are.'

One final point, 'The love I have for the game will never go.' And that's it, time's up on the interview. Coleman needs to check back in with his squad and resume his duties as captain. But before he departs, he asks: 'Did you get enough time?'

He will never change, always willing to give up his time for others.

25
Glenn Whelan

Stoke City (2008–17)

Games Played: 277

Goals Scored: 4

Assists Created: 12

Clean Sheets: 57

Yellow Cards: 44

Red Cards: 1

Wins: 96

Draws: 78

Losses: 103

Michael Tonge. Tom Soares. Seyi Olofinjana. Diego Arismendi. Dean Whitehead. Florent Cuvelier. Wilson Palacios. Maurice Edu. Charlie Adam. Steven Nzonzi. Stephen Ireland. Steve Sidwell. Giannelli Imbula. Joe Allen. Fourteen different players recruited over a nine-year period at an estimated cost of €80 million. Yet none of them could budge Glenn Whelan from the Stoke City midfield.

Every transfer window brought a new contender into the ThunderDome (or just Stoke's training ground in Clayton Wood). Two men enter, one man leaves. A tough-skinned Dubliner, Whelan fended off the attempts of men who hailed from ten different countries. They came from far and wide but none could displace him. He was always up for the fight, no matter the rival that Stoke's own MasterBlaster (aka manager Tony Pulis) put in front of him.

It was never personal for Whelan, yet then again it was. 'Any time there was a challenge I accepted it. It might have been easier for me to say: "I've had enough, I'm leaving." And I did have chances through the years to move to different clubs; they may not have been bigger and better than Stoke, it might have been more of a sideways step. But I saw it as a challenge. I can only speak highly of Tony Pulis. I spoke with him when he went on to West Brom and then Middlesbrough and he said that bringing those players in was as much about improving me as adding different options to the squad. He wanted me to keep my standards up and I was more than willing to accept the challenge. Stoke were always brilliant with me and I did get rewarded with new contracts to keep me at the club for a few extra years. But there would be times when you see new signings coming in and you're thinking "that's me gone". But I just looked at it that I had to change the manager's mind. I saw it that it was my jersey and if you want it then you're going to have to work for it.'

Whelan maintains that making it as a professional footballer is all about timing and luck. He didn't avail of either during his time at Manchester City when he first moved across to England in 2000 at the age of sixteen, but that just made him more determined to 'prove people wrong'. It wasn't so much a chip on his shoulder, but something quite a lot bigger. He felt like Sisyphus – from Greek mythology – who was condemned to roll a boulder up a hill only for it to roll back down every time he neared the top.

Whelan just couldn't understand why his efforts at Man City were being overlooked. Sure, there were seasoned professionals ahead of him, but none of his peers within the academy set-up and reserve team were better than him. Or at least that is how he felt. Two loan spells at Bury and being part of the Republic of Ireland squad that reached the last sixteen of the

2003 FIFA Under-20 World Youth Championship should have propelled him up the pecking order. And it did, to a degree, as he made the first-team bench a few times without ever appearing as a substitute. However, he wanted more and believed that he deserved more.

With a year left on his contract with Man City, Whelan met with the manager, Kevin Keegan, and made it clear that he was not prepared to sit around any longer. A mutual agreement was made to allow him to join Sheffield Wednesday in League One. That was the opportunity that he craved, the chance to show that he was ready for first-team football.

Within only a short space of time, anyone who had thought that Whelan's self-confidence was egotistical was, well, proved wrong. He adapted to the rigours of senior football straight away as his new club achieved promotion to the Championship and he continued his fine form in England's second tier. In those days, Whelan was more of a box-to-box midfielder and he netted eight goals in his third season with the Owls.

Complications soon set in as he delayed surgery on a hernia problem and then the club – or at least a former manager – wanted to cash in on him. Whelan just wanted to play football, so it was clear that the off-field shenanigans soured his time at Hillsborough. When the opportunity came to move, on his own terms, he joined Stoke City in the January transfer window in 2008 and helped them to achieve promotion. He was back in the Premier League.

Still, something didn't feel right. Whelan knew deep inside that he should have already been in that division, as a Man City player. And he was pretty frank about that when bumping into his former manager some years later. 'I saw him [Keegan] a couple of years ago and I said, more or less, that you made a boo-boo by letting me go. But I was going out to prove people wrong, I think that was always my mentality. It was always in the back of my mind [to get back to the Premier League]. There were lads there [at Man City] at the time, like Dickson Etuhu, Terry Dunfield and Joey Barton, and I felt that I was just as good as they were. You just want a manager or a coach to take some sort of chance on you when you're a young lad trying to break in. And that's all it can be down to. I don't think it was down to ability or the way I was as a person, it was just at that time the position I wanted to play in was heavily loaded.'

Despite the few words, Whelan doesn't hold any grudges towards Keegan. If he did then that bitterness might have derailed his career. Instead, he ultimately set his sights on looking forward. It is why he became such a consistent performer with Stoke City – racking up almost 300 Premier League games.

'I never thought I was going to be a Premier League player for however long I was, I was just grateful for every game that I did get to play,' he says. 'No matter what the manager or the analyst may say to you, you know the [calibre of] player that you are coming up against in every game. You know their weaknesses and their strengths. For instance, if it was [Steven] Gerrard, you had to be really close because you know he could score from forty yards or make a run into the box. As you go on, it's about your know-how and being prepared for each game.'

During his time with Stoke, they became known as a difficult team to play against. 'At Stoke, we had a way of playing, especially at home, that was about upsetting the bigger teams and stopping them from playing. The bigger teams definitely didn't like coming to play us but whenever we got a result against them it was earned because we would have out-worked them and out-fought them. I think we deserved more credit for some of our results. I know that Arsène Wenger [the former Arsenal manager] had a bee in his bonnet about how we played. But if you look back at the games [in which Stoke got results against Arsenal], on the day we were actually much better than them ... that may be tackling a bit harder or getting stuck in their face a little bit more. But there were a couple of games, I think under Mark Hughes, where we won 3-1 ... I think Bojan [Krkić, a graduate of the Barcelona youth academy, who played with Stoke between 2014 and 2018] got two ...

and it could have been five or six but he [Wenger] still came out and said we were physical. But if you look at the team sheet, we had Bojan and [Ibrahim] Afellay, [skilful] players like that. So it was a little bit of sour grapes on his part but we were always up for those games.'

Whelan epitomised that warrior spirit with his aggressive tackling, vital interceptions and knowing when to press an opponent. But it would be very unfair to typecast him as just a midfield disruptor. He didn't rack up ninety-one appearances for Ireland – taking in two UEFA European Championships – and outlast so many new signings at Stoke simply because he worked hard. No, he was much more than that. In fact, the records prove it.

After thirty years of the Premier League, Whelan is fifty-first in the all-time list of most passes completed. If that number doesn't strike you as being particularly high then consider that he is ahead of some world-class players who were synonymous with their passing ability, the likes of Mesut Özil, Paul Scholes, Scott Parker and Paul Pogba.

'People always say "you were safe [in his choice of pass], you were backwards, you were sideways" but, for me, I knew what I was in the team. That I had to get the ball to the better players, the more talented players, the ones who were going to create. That was my role. A lot of times, especially playing for my country under [Giovanni] Trapattoni, I was getting a lot of outside noise. But Trapattoni and Marco Tardelli, they were really pleased with me because that's what they wanted. What do I do? Do I keep the manager and assistant manager really happy? Or do I then try some more expansive passes just to keep some fans and a few critics off my back? I probably played the amount of games that I did because of being consistent in the role that the manager wanted me to do.

'And I was always in that role. If you look at my time with Ireland under Trapattoni, it was Keith [Andrews] who was given more rein to go forward when I had to stay closer to the centre-backs. It wasn't a case of mixing it up between us, I was the one who had to stay back. I remember one game when Trapattoni and Marco Tardelli were going absolutely bananas because I was ahead of Keith. That's just the way it was. I loved playing for my country, so if my manager asks me to do a role then that's what I'm going to do. It was the same at Stoke, I had a job to do for the team.'

Perhaps the perception of him would have changed had he been under managers with a different style. 'I would've loved to have had the chance to play in a proper footballing team who got it down and made six hundred passes per game. But that wasn't the case with Tony Pulis at Stoke and Trapattoni with Ireland. There is no doubt that I would have loved to have played alongside a [Paul] Scholes, [Steven] Gerrard or [Frank] Lampard, because I knew that I was good at getting the ball and giving it to better players. If you look at the Man City team now, if you had myself in the middle as the anchor and you had [Kevin] De Bruyne and Bernardo Silva on either side, there is no doubt that you would be looked at as a better player. But it was the case that the style of football with the teams that I played for was different.'

Some people may think that Whelan is getting slightly above himself with comments like that, but when one observes his overall play during his best years it is far from an exaggeration to suggest that he could have fitted into any of the top Premier League teams. Just look at his numbers: in the 2015–16 season, he had a ninety per cent pass completion rate, he won over half his duels, he made 365 interceptions and slid the ball forward 847 times with progressive forward passes.

Cynics may suggest that his running stats would let him down in this debate. But this is football, not athletics. He didn't need to make long sprints but rather short, sharp bursts to cover ground, to press the ball or to make space to receive a pass. Whelan has always been an intelligent footballer and it is why he has a lot of the qualities required to become an excellent coach. He doesn't care for buzz words or someone trying to be better than they are just to impress others. He believes in simplicity, in discipline and in using the ball.

Even when he left Stoke to drop down to the Championship with Aston Villa in 2017, he was still an influential player and helped them to seal promotion back to the Premier League. He would go on to play for Hearts, Fleetwood Town and Bristol Rovers as his playing days stretched on, but rarely would you ever see him misplace a pass or be caught in possession of the ball. Even an aging fox knows their way around the chicken coop.

Whelan is, and should be, proud of his impact on the Premier League. And history should be kind in remembering him as one of the best Irish midfielders to grace the league.

26
Matt Doherty

Wolverhampton Wanderers (2011–12, 2018–20), Tottenham Hotspur (2020–Present)

Games Played: 107

Goals Scored: 10

Assists Created: 14

Clean Sheets: 24

Yellow Cards: 8

Red Cards: 1

Wins: 51

Draws: 27

Losses: 29

Matt Doherty became a fan favourite at Wolverhampton Wanderers before moving to Tottenham Hotspur. It has always been a motivation to see how high he can go in the Premier League. Doherty's unique insights into his journey are searingly honest and incredibly informative of just what an Irish player has to go through in order to thrive in the 'best league in the world'.

From kicking a ball against a wall in the Dublin suburb of Swords to being José Mourinho's top summer target, he has come a long way. And there is still more to come.

What are your earliest memories of the Premier League?

I used to go with my dad down to the pub to watch games and then we got a box where you had to enter in channel 433 to get the 12.30 game. I just remember that if you played in the Premier League it was the best thing that you could ever achieve, so that was always the dream.

Was the decision to join Belvedere, Ireland's top schoolboy team at the time, influenced by chasing that Premier League dream?

The team that we had at Home Farm, where I was playing, weren't great and I think my dad liked the coaches at Belvedere. Maybe he saw a route towards international [squads] but I didn't play a lot of international football at underage.

Then I went to Bohemians after that. I was meant to go to Sporting Fingal. The coach [Liam Buckley] was a really nice man and they were meant to be doing things properly as a club. But then they had financial problems and my dad was speaking to Pat Fenlon, who wanted to bring me to Bohs.

The Premier League was still on my mind then but the path to get there wasn't as clear. My thought process there was that I would have to try to get away from the League of Ireland by the time I was twenty-one. I hadn't actually played much for Bohs but then I played in a pre-season friendly against Wolves and Mick McCarthy saw me play. The chips just fell into place and it was right place, right time kind of thing. But, in saying that, you still have to perform or do something that catches their eye.

Once you get there, the whole start of trying to break through with reserve team football … there is so much that goes with it when you think about it. People just think, 'Oh, you went over, grew up a little bit and then you play.' But that is so far from what actually happens.

How were those early years at Wolves?

I played reserve team football and it was fine, it's part of the trade that you have to do to get better. From early on, I was around the first team, travelling to games, being in the stands at times, and they were in the Premier League at the time so that was a good buzz. You're also thinking that if you make the bench you get a little bonus, so you couldn't be happier at being involved.

Do you remember the first time you got a bonus payment?
Yeah, we were playing Blackburn away and I was wearing mouldies [plastic or rubber studded football boots]. I was on the bench and went out to warm up, but as a defender you can't be wearing mouldies, that's a no-go. A few of the players were like, 'Don't let the gaffer see those.' They were half-joking but now that I know Mick [McCarthy] they were probably being serious.

But just by making the bench I got a bonus. I think it was around £2,500. I was only eighteen so that made a huge difference. I didn't go crazy but it did get spent.

Did that bonus payment open your eyes to the amount of money that is involved in the Premier League?
Not really. The money side of it didn't really come into effect until I was four or five contracts in. You haven't done anything up to that point. But then you get agents to negotiate on your behalf. People think that money is all that you think about as a footballer but you don't. If they offer you something and it's the going rate, then that's the going rate.

When I was at Wolves, when I first went there, I was earning £500 a week. Then a year they come back and say here's £1,200 [a week] and you're like 'yeah, grand'. You're not driven by money at all.

When you go on in your career, you want to be valued. You don't want to be ripped off with anything, like you don't in life anyway. And you want your abilities to be valued. Whatever the going rate for that is then that's what it is. If you're able to get a bit more, you work a bit harder. Nobody sits down and says 'Here's a load of money.' That's why everything is structured, you build your way up and then eventually fall into where you're meant to be.

A lot of cynics will suggest that you left Wolverhampton Wanderers to sign for Tottenham Hotspur because you were getting more money. How does that make you feel?

Yeah, it's easy to say that. That is a part of it also and it is part of the industry. If someone is here [Doherty places his hand at medium height) then they want to get to here [raising hand to a higher level]. But first of all, José [Mourinho] was the manager and it would've been silly to say no to him. And he really wanted me. He told me that I was his number one choice to come in. He even said to me that if the chairman came to him and said that he could only have one signing in the summer, I was the only one he wanted. So who would say no to that?

Spurs are a huge club, the training ground, the stadium, possibly fighting for Champions League football. I had run my course at Wolves. I wanted to try and leave that summer anyway, whether it was Tottenham or not. I had been there for so long. I think I would have regretted staying there for longer. Every player is different.

Even when things were not going well [at Tottenham] I still didn't regret it. I was happy to make the step. It's a bit of an ego thing as well, isn't it? You want to say that you've played for a top team. Tottenham choose eleven players every week, who are all top players, and you are one of those players. That gives you a good feeling.

My dad didn't love the move for me. He would probably have had me stay at Wolves, but how could I say no? I probably could've gone back to Wolves and said 'give me a second contract' but I didn't want to do that. And I saw stuff saying about going back in the January, but I didn't want to do that either [there was speculation that Wolves were attempting to re-sign Doherty on loan in the January transfer window in 2022]. I had a great time at Wolves but I think if I went back … you should never really go back …

Did the experience of working with José Mourinho live up to what you thought it was going to be?

I let him down. People think that he was bad for me but it was the other way round. He put a lot of faith in me and I didn't really perform. I just didn't play well, I just didn't grasp it … I don't know, I just wasn't able to get going there at the start.

The shape was obviously different [from Wolves]. The difference was that at Tottenham they have so much ability going forward, with the players that they have, that maybe I wasn't necessarily needed to play high and create stuff. So my main job was maybe just to be a defender. But my game is about going forward.

To be fair to José, they tried to play me high but it wasn't working for the team, we were leaving too many spaces. I just didn't perform for him. He's a great guy … I could sit here with him now and have dinner with him and have the best time ever. I spoke to him a few times about it, but I don't know what it was. It's a bit of a regret that I wasn't able to perform like how he saw me in his head.

How did you feel when the criticism came? That people suggested it was too high a jump for you to make.

I know that I'm good enough. I have the ability and I have what it takes to be able to play, so I never doubted that in my mind. But it was a case of 'Is it too late to make the step up?' I thought that was possible, that my opportunity could have been gone. I didn't fear the January window but I wasn't getting that much game-time so I did think that going somewhere for six months might refresh me. But I wasn't thinking that the club were looking to sell me or anything like that.

But everyone has a price. Even if you are playing well, you could still move on. It could be something that benefits you. But at no point have I not enjoyed going to work. Like I said earlier with the ego thing, you want to play every game and try to make a difference, especially when the team is struggling.

After José Mourinho left Tottenham, you were reunited with your old Wolves manager Nuno Espírito Santo. It seemed like he was the man who could get the best out of you?

I was a bit unfortunate with Nuno at the start because I picked up COVID in the middle of pre-season. I came back and we played Chelsea in pre-season and I was playing right-back. Then we were playing Arsenal on the Sunday. But because I had had COVID, after the Chelsea game I had to do a few extra runs because I had missed a lot of training, and I just felt a little twinge in my hamstring. On the Sunday against Arsenal, it was a case of just sit it out and [Japhet] Tanganga played and he played really well so he started the first game of the season. So if I didn't do those runs then I might have played the first game of the season and things might have been different.

All of the managers that I've had [at club level] have been so different. Nuno got the best out of me at Wolves and Antonio [Conte] has been getting the best out of me [at Spurs]. Maybe the common denominator is the formation. I seem to thrive a lot in the wing-back position. I'm not all about burning past people, it's more about my timing and using my brain to see spaces or certain gaps. So I think the shape of the team helps me to do what I do.

What about the demands of playing in the wing-back position?

People think of a wing-back as a high, wide person just running. But you have to defend and attack. You're usually playing against full-backs and wingers who are usually the quickest or the trickiest players on the pitch. You have to obviously be fit and be able to get up and down [the line]. You have to contribute offensively in terms of goals, assists and stuff like that because that is the whole point of the position. Then you have to defend, like at the back post. So it is a specialised position. I don't know how we stumbled upon it but I guess as a defender who loves to attack it is kind of perfect. Defensively, I'm more confident in that position because in my head I know that if something happens and I'm out of the game, there is another centre-back already there. So you play with a bit more courage because you know there is a bit more cover behind you.

You should want that responsibility and it's a big responsibility. To play for a club like Tottenham should make you proud. With a club of that size and the players they try to recruit, you can feel the pressure. When you're in that big stadium, you really feel that you have to win the game. There is no 'oh we lost, it's fine, we'll go win next week', there is a proper inquest if you lose a game.

Have you ever felt an inferiority complex about being Irish within a squad of so many international star players?
Not really. I think that kind of stuff comes from the outside. But maybe Irish players don't get the credit that they deserve at times. If you look at Seamus [Coleman], how many players has he fended off at Everton? All throughout his career he has consistently been there and proved that he is a great player. When Everton brought in [Djibril] Sidibé everyone was saying that it was end of Seamus. But he just kept doing what he has always done and is still playing now. If you look at it from another way, like if Seamus had come from abroad, from somewhere like Benfica, then people would be talking about him in a different way. It's strange, isn't it?

You have to have an ego, you just wouldn't survive at big clubs if you didn't have it. I wouldn't say that I was proud to have one, you just build it up. To get to that point you must be good at something. Whether you are being ruthless or selfish or if you really believe that you are the best at what you do and it should be you no matter what – whether that is the case or not, you still believe it.

How do you find the work/life balance, especially after your career reached a higher level?

Being a footballer every day, I think it has made me cold in certain aspects. In family life I'm just emotionless at times. In football you have to stay so level that I take that across into family life at times and that's not really a great thing.

Obviously you love your kids but I just know from people telling me that I'm quite emotionless, quite cold. People used to say that I was never like that but in my head that is just the way it has to be. If someone was to come up and ask for a picture, I'd say yeah but my face would not change. So I'm not deliberately doing that ... I don't know how to explain it ... I'm just not overly friendly. I like the people who are close to me, who I trust, but I don't welcome in that many.

It probably stems from bad times. You know when you're having bad times in the Premier League and the scrutiny is high, you literally don't want to go out. You are just miserable. And in the Premier League you can be on that slippery slope for a while because it's so hard. Maybe it has just stuck. For me, I feel like I've always been that way, but people have said that I've changed. Even if I'm playing bad or good, I'm still quite the same, I'm still cold. I'm just being honest.

Do you think that will change when you finish playing football? That it will be a release of pressure.

Maybe. But people say that should happen when you have kids but I'm just the same. Maybe it's just my personality. It's not a horrendous thing, it's just sometimes that I'm cold towards people. Maybe it is being part of a high-level environment, having that killer [instinct] in you because you are competing against people trying to take your place. That can change your whole career and that can then change everything.

If you feel that you come across as cold, and others perceive you as being quite laid-back, has that ever caused you a problem in such a demanding environment as the Premier League?

I know what you mean. Some people might look at me and think I'm not arsed but that is just my running style. It looks like I'm just jogging at times but I'm actually not. So I can understand if a manager thinks that there is no intensity to what I'm doing or that I don't seem to care. But I think that has been misinterpreted a lot.

That's probably why you don't get the credit that you deserve. They probably don't like you before they like you, so there might be a bit of that. I think the real top managers they understand, they see what it is. My style has never changed, it has always looked like 'Do I have another gear?' or 'Am I really giving everything?'

But I am. I am giving everything.

How do you handle the criticism that comes via social media?

There comes a time when you turn off the notifications, whether they are good or bad. Sometimes you go on your socials and you're not looking for anything and then you see a photo of yourself, you click on it and it says something like 'worst signing ever'. So you've seen it by not even looking for it.

I'm more disciplined with my time when I go on social media. If you lose and play bad then I'm not going to go straight on it. Why do that to yourself? It feels like sports is the only industry where you can get abuse and it's okay.

What would a successful Premier League career be for you?

Just to play as many games as possible, to play in the Champions League. It's already a huge privilege for me to have worked with José and Conte, who are two of the best managers ever. Yeah, just play as many games as possible, to realise that dream of playing in the Champions League, try to win a trophy and to feel that I belong there.

In my first year in the Premier League, I went on holidays, I went to Barbados, and somebody recognised me. That wouldn't have happened if I was in the Championship. But the Premier League is on channels that we don't even know about. It's so global. I've noticed that a lot more at Tottenham, as we would go most places and there would be Tottenham fans there. It reminds me of how big the Premier League is.

27
Mark Travers

Bournemouth (2018–2020, 2022–Present)
Games Played: 3
Clean Sheets: 0
Yellow Cards: 1
Red Cards: 0
Wins: 1
Draws: 0
Losses: 2

As soon as the phone call ended, the panic set in. The Travers family were on the clock. Michael and Louise had to secure flights, hotels and transfers to London and then to England's south coast in record time. It was like a scene from *Planes, Trains and Automobiles*. Except they were not rushing home for Thanksgiving but rather desperate to be there for their son's Premier League debut.

It was early afternoon on 3 May 2019 when Mark Travers phoned home and delivered his parents the news that Bournemouth manager Eddie Howe had just given him: he would be in the starting line-up for their game at home to Tottenham Hotspur the next day.

With the season drawing to a close and Bournemouth comfortable with their league position, they decided to see how their rookie goalkeeper would fare in the heat of battle in the Premier League. It was no-lose situation for them, and a win-win for the nineteen-year-old.

Reliving the experience, Travers says: 'Eddie Howe pulled me on the Friday before training to tell me that I was going to start. It was an unreal feeling, to be honest. I wasn't expecting it. I was just grateful to get an opportunity. I tried to take it as best as I could. It was a twelve-thirty kick-off on a Saturday so I didn't have much time to think about it – I just got up, went in to the stadium and started to feel the atmosphere. It probably didn't feel real in the moment that is was happening but afterwards, when all of your friends and family are texting you, it's a great buzz and one that I'll always remember.

'I had been third choice for probably two seasons, being part of the squad, travelling to all of the games and trying to do all of the right things. I think the manager probably saw that and wanted to give me an opportunity to play a game and see what I was like,' he says. 'I didn't know how it would go, I just wanted to repay the manager as best as I could with a good performance. Tottenham played Ajax in the Champions League semi-final earlier that week and I remember thinking that it would be great to play against a team like that. Then come the weekend I'm playing against them, which was class. They had a forward line of Son [Heung-min], Dele Alli and Lucas Moura. Harry Kane was out injured that day. Before every game a goalkeeper has a little preview of what they are going to face, the attacking threats that will come from the forward line and they had some forward line.

'When you watch football for so long you kind of know what most players are about in the Premier League, but I quickly found out on match-day that those players could do anything … whether it was using their right or left foot, how they turn, the decisions they make. So it was great to have information going into the game, but you have to go off how the game goes. I just tried to chill out and enjoy the experience because it is very rare that anyone gets that opportunity and I was buzzing to get it. The manager helped to put me at ease by telling me that I deserved the chance and then the information from the goalkeeping coaches about trusting in the work that we had done all season helped massively.'

Summarising what constitutes a great game for a goalkeeper is a tricky one. A statistician might point to a clean sheet as a clear indicator of a solid performance: 0 goals conceded + 90 minutes = 9/10. However, a clean sheet can be achieved through the opposition being toothless in attack or a defence being outstanding or even a goalkeeper being incredibly lucky. What works better is seeing a goalkeeper make saves, react under pressure and get back up when truly tested under pressure. That is what Travers showed in that 1-0 win over Tottenham.

'Luckily, I got a chance to make some saves, but, to be honest, there was one chance early on from Lucas Moura ... I had a high starting position and I think he won a tackle on the half-way line and shot and he nearly dinked me from about fifty yards. So that was a quick reminder of what the level was that I was playing at ... and it made me drop off a few yards,' he remembers. It was my first Premier League game so I wanted to show what I could do and prove myself. As a goalkeeper there are loads of different ways to have a good game ... it could be having a good presence in your box, coming for crosses, having good distribution or making a few saves. I had a few shots to handle, which was good in one way because there can be a lot of games where you have little to do. But I got to show that I was capable of making saves when called upon.'

Those saves were quite something. He denied Alli with a diving effort to his right, before shutting out Moura on three occasions, including an acrobatic movement to palm a header over the crossbar. It was seriously impressive stuff for the first teenage keeper to start in the Premier League in over a decade, following on from Joe Hart's debut for Manchester City in 2006.

The reaction to Travers's performance was hard to ignore. The Bournemouth fans chanted 'Super Keeper' until their throats went dry, he was voted the official Man of the Match, the media queued up for post-match interviews with him and he was profiled on *Match of the Day*. A new Premier League star had been born ... or at least, finally, discovered.

So how did he feel after it all?

'Once I got a taste for it I wanted more games to come. But we had just one more game because it was the end of the season. Still, I got to experience it and that was great for me,' he says. 'Coming from Ireland, and from Maynooth, you don't hear too much of young lads getting to play in the Premier League so it was great to represent my country and my home town.'

It's interesting that Travers mentions Maynooth, a sleepy town in north County Kildare with a population just shy of 15,000 where the local university and the Carton House Hotel and Golf Club are the big attractions. It is not a place known for producing footballers and Travers knew from early on that a move away from playing with his friends at the local club in Confey would have to come if he was to fulfil his potential.

After a stint with Lucan United, just over the Dublin border, he then moved to Shamrock Rovers to be part of their upgraded underage structure. It was around this time that he started to receive call-ups for Republic of Ireland teams and benefit from specialised goalkeeping coaching – specifically from the vastly experienced Dermot O'Neill, who was juggling roles with Ireland Under-17s and Rovers at the same time.

Whispers began to circulate around the Irish football community that there was a special talent coming through who could potentially become Ireland's Number 1. Bournemouth didn't wait around and signed him up as quickly as possible. The kid from Maynooth was being given a chance.

Travers joined Bournemouth in the summer of 2016, a year after the club had achieved promotion to the Premier League for the first time. He knew that a breakthrough to the first team would take some time, but he was prepared to work hard, listen to his coaches and be patient. There were long bus journeys, and sometimes short flights, that took him up and down England. Each time, he packed his boots and his gloves, knowing that he would not see any game-time. But he still had to prepare as best he could, for appearances more than anything. If the manager ever caught a glimpse of him, Travers had to be seen to be as professional as possible. That was never going to be a problem, though, considering that he is a polite, respectful young man with a shy demeanour and a serious work ethic.

Still, he had to wait his turn. Bournemouth sent him twenty-five miles up the road to Dorset to join non-league Weymouth for a loan spell. It was meant to be a low-key introduction to senior football but Travers spoiled that by scoring on his debut. Yes, his first game at senior level saw him become a goalscoring goalkeeper!

Not many people expected much when he stepped up to take a free-kick thirty yards from his own goal line, but Travers's power sent the ball long and over the head of the Bishop's Stortford keeper to help them win 3-2 away from home.

By the way, if it ever comes up in a pub quiz, be aware that Travers became just the third Irish goalkeeper to score a goal in English football, following on from Seamus McDonagh for Bolton Wanderers and Barry Roche for Morecambe.

It wasn't that goal, however, that would have influenced Bournemouth scouts to send glowing reports back to Howe about their teenage keeper. At 6ft 3in, he was learning how best to use his frame: his aerial dominance improved with each game, his anticipation and reading of the game was excellent, his shot-stopping was top-notch, his kicking was direct and his confidence was growing. He was certainly better than non-league, but was he ready for the Premier League?

After the Weymouth loan and two games in the Premier League (he shipped five goals in his next game away to Crystal Palace), Travers hoped that he would move up the pecking order for the 2019–20 season. Except Artur Boruc and Aaron Ramsdale were ahead of him. One appearance in that campaign made it a frustrating one, especially since the Cherries suffered relegation to the Championship.

Patience, once again, was what Bournemouth asked from him. Howe had departed, with his former assistant Jason Tindall taking over. Travers was seen as the back-up choice to Asmir Begović with Boruc and Ramsdale now gone. A loan spell to Swindon Town in League One was meant to sate his appetite for game-time but he was recalled after just eight games to sit on the Bournemouth bench again. Patience, patience.

It wasn't until the next summer, when Scott Parker was appointed as the new manager, that a route back to the Premier League and regular playing time felt achievable to Travers. The new boss placed his trust in him and was rewarded with twenty clean sheets from forty-five games in a promotion-winning season. Everything had changed. 'Coming into the last pre-season, I was really unsure of what was going to happen. Then the new manager came in and gave me an opportunity, which was class. He stood by me through the whole season and I'm very grateful for that. That match-day experience is something that I needed to get more of.

'Confidence is a big part of it,' explains Travers. 'I had to learn how to build that confidence of becoming the starting goalkeeper after going from being the Number 2 or Number 3 keeper. From that first game in the Premier League to now I have gained a lot of experience, but I still have loads to learn and need to keep working hard to get even better.'

Now he has a return to the Premier League to look forward to. 'Being a Premier League Number 1,' he says, 'is something that I've always tried to work towards. It's something that I always dreamed of as a kid. But I can't take anything for granted because you constantly have to prove yourself and rise to the challenge of playing in the Premier League.'

Travers now believes that he is ready to become a Premier League regular. However, things could have been altogether different if he had chosen another path in his early teenage years, when a career in golf was an option. A member at Carton House, Travers was identified as someone who could possibly go professional. So he had a decision to make: football or golf?

'Football was always the number one focus. Golf is a really tough sport to crack, the level and quality is so high that it is so difficult to pursue a career in it. Football likewise. But being part of a team sport was a big factor for me,' he says. 'Football was the main focus come fifteen, sixteen, but I did love the golf as well. When I started to get trials with clubs in England, that was probably when I made my choice. It would be around that age that aspiring golfers would try to get scholarships to America but I don't know if I would have been at that level.'

Travers laughs at the suggestion that a second career in golf might be in his future. His membership at Carton House has long since lapsed, but maybe they will honour him with a life-time membership if he does become a Premier League star.

One thing that is for sure, his parents won't fret about missing out on seeing their son realise his dream. They made it in time for his debut and can now look forward to many more memorable days watching him shut out some of the best strikers in the world.

28
John Egan

Sheffield United (2019–21)

Games Played: 67

Goals Scored: 2

Assists Created: 1

Clean Sheets: 16

Yellow Cards: 10

Red Cards: 2

Wins: 19

Draws: 13

Losses: 35

'I always had an unwavering belief that I would play in the Premier League.'

Out on the local green, John Egan viewed every game through the eyes of an established Premier League footballer. Every tackle was combative. Every goal scored was glorious. Every moment was impactful. Right up until he was called in for his dinner, that is.

Every day was about playing football. Every day was about playing out that fantasy. As soon as he had raced home from school, it was out to his very own theatre of dreams. Come rain, hail or sunshine, Egan was there with his friends to play the beautiful game in the most beautiful way.

The surroundings of Bishopstown, a lively suburb in the south-west of Cork City, might not have been the amphitheatre that he saw in his mind's eye but all it really needed to be was a lump of grass steady enough to withstand a dozen kids trampling all over it. The other playground of choice was the Bishopstown GAA club, where he followed in the giant shadow of his father, John Snr. A six-time All-Ireland winner with Kerry, his father was one of the very few men to be royally welcomed over the Cork–Kerry border, such was his glowing reputation as a legendary sportsman and respectable member of the local Gardaí.

Egan lived something of a double life throughout his youth. One life looked destined to follow a similar trajectory as his father in becoming a star of Gaelic games (he was just as good with a hurley and a sliotar as he was with a football). The other was on the soccer field, where he was excelling with Greenwood FC and earning call-ups to Republic of Ireland underage squads.

A decision had to be made. A hard decision. GAA or soccer? He didn't want to disappoint his father, but then again his father never put any pressure on him to do anything other than what he enjoyed most. That made it easy: it was soccer.

It helped that scouts were making regular visits to Greenwood to nod simultaneously in acknowledgement of every good thing that Egan did on the pitch. They all wanted to capture his signature, but it was Sunderland who eventually succeeded.

Swapping the comforts of home for an unknown world in the north-east of England wasn't easy. He had to leave behind family, friends and everything that he knew. Egan, though, has always been a strong-minded person, unafraid of making big decisions.

As for his time with the Black Cats, it's probably best to allow Egan tell the story: 'I started getting on the bench when I was nineteen,' he says. 'My first game [on the bench] was away to Manchester United at Old Trafford in November 2011 in the Premier League. On the Friday before I had been training with the first team, in the way that reserve team players make up the numbers sometimes, and then out of nowhere the reserve team manager Keith Birken rang me and said "You're travelling with the first team." I was absolutely buzzing. I didn't get on that day but it was still an unbelievable experience. Actually, James McClean was on the bench that day as well. I got on the bench again against Fulham the following week. Something happened with Michael Turner during the game, I think it was his nose, and the manager Steve Bruce told me to get warmed up. I was running up and down the sideline, constantly looking back to see if they were about to call my name. But Turner was a tough man and played on, so it wasn't to be for me.'

Martin O'Neill replaced Bruce as Sunderland boss after the next game and he had his own plans, which didn't include Egan. (Ironically it would be O'Neill who would give the Cork native his Republic of Ireland senior debut six years later, but in 2011 he viewed him as just another rookie defender.) 'I think I was close to making my debut under Steve Bruce but then he left the club and everything changed. Other managers wanted to go with more experienced players and we were fighting to stay in the Premier League so that was fair enough. But it meant that I was back at the start.'

Egan understood it. Sure, he felt ready to compete for a place in the first team, although the likes of John O'Shea, Wes Brown, Michael Turner, Titus Bramble and Matthew Kilgallon were ahead of him in the pecking order. He needed games to prove himself and that is exactly what he went in search of.

Once the January transfer window opened in 2012, he went on loan to Crystal Palace in the Championship but only registered one game there. Two months later he tried again, this time with Sheffield United, but it was the same result.

Only the previous summer, Egan had captained the Ireland Under-19s to the semi-finals of the UEFA Under-19 European Championships. Surely he deserved a better chance than what was coming his way? He returned to Sunderland, played reserve team football and waited for the pre-season to properly audition for O'Neill.

The opportunity arrived during a tour of South Korea, where he featured twice in a pre-season tournament. Yet the manager still opted to replace the outgoing Turner with Spanish centre-back Carlos Cuéllar. Egan knew that another loan spell was needed; this time, however, he would drop to League One in order to ensure game-time.

In November, he joined Bradford City and everything started well with three games and his confidence building. Then, in the fourth game against Plymouth Argyle, he suffered a broken leg that would put him out of action for a year. Yet again, so close, but so far.

That was a tough year for Egan as, in April, he had lost his father. If he started to have doubts about fulfilling his ambition to play in the Premier League at that point, they would have been understandable. A return home to Bishopstown, where a shot with the Cork county team would be a possibility, was an option. Nobody would have deemed him a failure. After all, ninety-nine per cent of academy players don't make the grade in professional football. He had a decision to make.

Except Egan saw it only one way – he would do everything possible to make it as a footballer. 'I wouldn't have continued to play football if I didn't believe that I could do well. The ambition was always to play in the Premier League and to play for my country. That's what keeps you going through the hard times, believing in that and believing in yourself,' reaffirms Egan. 'Deep down, when I was on my way back from that injury, I knew that when I came back that I would have to prove myself all over again. I didn't play a first-team game for about fourteen months. I knew that I had to get a lot of games under my belt before I could start moving up the leagues again.

'For any young player when you get to nineteen, twenty, I think Under-20 or Under-23 football isn't ideal. You need to get out and play at first-team level somewhere, anywhere. You need to make a career for yourself, so you should go out quickly. When you do play regularly at first-team level then there should be no going back to the Under-23s. I looked at the likes of Jordan Pickford and Jordan Henderson, who went out, played a lot of games and came back with real confidence in themselves. They broke into the first team at Sunderland and then went on to other clubs. They are examples of what I saw at first hand. So I think when you do get that experience you are a different player.'

Motivated by what fellow academy graduates Pickford and Henderson had achieved, Egan decided to leave Sunderland behind to join Gillingham in League One – two tiers below the Premier League. It was the equivalent of taking two steps back in order to, eventually, make a giant leap forward.

Earlier in the season, he had benefited from a loan spell at Southend United, where he played thirteen games. That alerted Gillingham boss Peter Taylor to his talents. Egan wasted little time in signing a two-year deal, which made the summer of 2014 the one when he really got going with his professional career.

The journey from Sunderland to Gillingham is nearly 500 kilometres and takes around five hours by car. The gap between the two clubs in 2014 was thirty-eight places, from the Premier League through the Championship down to League One. It was a long way for Egan to go in order to make the ultimate comeback.

'In my mind, going to Gillingham was that giant leap forward. I may have been at a Premier League club in Sunderland but I hadn't been playing in the Premier League. Gillingham put a lot of faith in me, I think I played near to fifty games in my first season, so it was by far the most games I had played up to that date and I was still only twenty-one, twenty-two at the time,' says Egan. 'It was really enjoyable and a great experience. We just missed out on the play-offs in my second season but if we didn't have a couple of injuries to key players then we might have got promoted.'

Soon Egan found himself moving up the ladder anyway. 'Then Brentford came in for me and that was exciting. They are very thorough in their signings, they are a well-run club and it was a no-brainer for me as they were in the Championship at the time. I learned a lot from playing in a really good team under a really good manager in Dean Smith. Brentford was perfect for me in many ways and I thought that my route to the Premier League was going to be with them, but it didn't happen during my time. We went close but missed out. And when Sheffield United came in that was a tough decision to make because they were flying and I was happy with Brentford. But I was really excited by what Sheffield United were doing, the players they had, the manager and I felt that they had a really good chance of getting promoted to the Premier League. Promotion in my first season there was special and it's been the best part of my career to date being with Sheffield United.'

From Gillingham in League One to Sheffield United in the Premier League within five years. Egan's decision-making had paid off.

That first year as a Premier League player in 2019 was indeed special. Sheffield United finished ninth after seeing their unique style of play – which consisted of overlapping centre-backs – produce big results away to Chelsea and at home to Arsenal, Manchester United and Tottenham Hotspur. As a defender, Egan was the one chosen to mind the house whenever his fellow centre-backs Jack O'Connell and Chris Basham tore off on their overlapping runs forward. Not that he minded. 'I think I would have had to be taken off at half-time such was the amount of running that the boys did galloping around the pitch,' laughs Egan.

Even though he had achieved what he set out to, there was little time for Egan to bask in the experience of being a Premier League footballer, as there was work to do. 'When you're in the middle of it you're just thinking about the next challenge or the next game. We knew coming into the Premier League that our style of play would cause problems. We had belief in ourselves, even if a lot of us were going into the unknown. In our first game, against Bournemouth, we got a last-minute equaliser and that was huge for our confidence,' says Egan. 'There were some really big highs that season and it really was special, because we had a really good team, some really good lads in the dressing room and we played some good football too. We were up in fifth and sixth spot with only a few games to go in the season, but we lost the last three. So we almost made Europe in our first year up in the Premier League.

'Personally, it was a really good season. I scored my first Premier League goal against Burnley on the Saturday and then three or four days later I scored the winner against Wolves. In the space of a few days I had scored two big goals for the club and two big goals for myself. That was an unbelievable feeling.

'Sometimes it hits you when you are going out to play against Liverpool, Man United or Man City. And the lads in a group chat from back home might send through a picture of you standing alongside someone like [Sergio] Aguero. It's probably more surreal for them because when you are in the thick of it you just want to compete and prove that you are a Premier League player.'

Egan certainly proved that with sixty-seven games accumulated over two seasons before Sheffield United were relegated. Now he starts over once again, attempting to get back to the Premier League.

29
Enda Stevens

Aston Villa (2012–13), Sheffield United (2019–21)

Games Played: 75

Goals Scored: 2

Assists Created: 5

Clean Sheets: 16

Yellow Cards: 14

Red Cards: 0

Wins: 20

Draws: 16

Losses: 39

The ambition was to get to the Premier League and the journey began with lung-bursting laps around 'the Bogies'. Officially, it is named Pope John Paul Park, but locals in Cabra, west Dublin, would raise a confused eyebrow if you used that title when asking for directions. Ask them how to get to the Bogies, though, and they will be only too happy to point the way. There is nothing spectacular about it, it's just another public park. Yet this is where one of the country's nine FAI–ETB courses is run. Inside the Parkside Community and Sports Centre, a classroom is set up, changing rooms are prepared and the kettle is on the boil. The students are not really students at all, but footballers aspiring to forge a career in the professional game. That was why Enda Stevens signed up.

Hailing from Drimnagh on the southside of Dublin, Stevens should probably have attended the centre in Ringsend. But a couple of friends were going to Cabra so he tagged along. Little did he know at the time that it would help to creak open the door of opportunity to become a full-time footballer.

The Cabra course was run by Harry McCue and Gino Brazil – two League of Ireland stalwarts with a reputation of being hard but fair in their development of players. They created an environment that brought the best out in teenagers who may have 'missed the boat' when it came to getting a move abroad to England.

Usually the first step was to help them find a club in the League of Ireland. Stevens was one of many to benefit from this. He had played a little for UCD, but soon after he had joined the course an offer came through from St Patrick's Athletic. This was the start of it all. This was what all those mornings jogging around the Bogies were meant to lead to.

'It's probably the most fun I've ever had – on that ETB course. I was surrounded by a lot of good people and it was probably the time of my life,' says Stevens. 'The course is there to get you into that culture of training and learning. I was able to get the best of both with the training and competitive games with St Pat's and the classwork with the ETB. That course gets you into the mindset of being a professional.'

Stevens's star was on the rise. After just one season with St Pat's he switched to Shamrock Rovers and was immediately thrust into a league-winning side. A break through to the UEFA Europa League followed and the defender's performances helped to rev up the hype machine as rumours of English clubs monitoring his progress started to swirl.

Within days of a famous victory over Partizan Belgrade, the rumours morphed into enquiries from interested clubs. There was one Championship club and one Premier League club keen on the full-back. But everything changed when Stevens was informed by his agent that Aston Villa had suddenly entered the fray.

For the Dubliner there wasn't really a decision to make because Villa were a big Premier League club; it was simply a case of how quickly he could sign the forms to become a Villa player. And the club were keen to get things done promptly too, as the transfer deadline was fast approaching.

Stevens scribbled his signature on the contract to become a Premier League player – though it was agreed that he would finish the season with Rovers first and then move over to Birmingham in January. Everything was set up nicely.

When he eventually got to Villa, however, it was not what he was expecting. The club were scrapping for top-flight survival, so the atmosphere was quite tense. He also went into the reserve team squad, not the first-team squad. 'It was a different culture,' explains Stevens. 'At Rovers you are a tight-knit gang, you are a close-knit dressing room, and then you go over to England and it's not that same feel. There were great people in the Villa changing room but it was a different feel.'

Stevens found it difficult to settle. 'I never had a taste of a top-level culture before. Obviously these players were on a lot of money, it's flashy. And you have so many different personalities, you've got French, English, Dutch, and I would never have been in that kind of environment. It was a shock. When I arrived over the club was in a relegation scrap, so chances of playing straight away weren't great. Maybe there were some opportunities where I could have played but there was so much at stake with Aston Villa then that I don't think it was ever a case of throwing me in.

'There was a change of manager in the summer. I came back, had a good pre-season, played in a cup game, got injured, then came back from injury and had to wait for my chance. We played Sunderland away in the Premier League and two left-backs got injured in the one game and that's when my opportunity came. It's a tough one because when I look back at it, I don't think I was ready to sustain a Premier League career with the way I was performing. But in that moment I thought I was doing okay, enough to play more in that season. I think I played five games on the bounce and then got injured. When I came back I never really reached the level of performance that was needed from me. My chance was gone then, that was it done.'

Stevens felt that one mistake under manager Paul Lambert was enough to end his days in a Villa jersey. That is how ruthless it can be at that level, where managers are constantly in fear of being fired so they rarely take a chance of younger players who lack experience. Welcome to the Premier League!

Once he found himself on the outside looking in, there were two options available: 1) Stick around and play Under-23 football, 2) Go out on loan to a lower division and play first-team football. Stevens opted for the latter option, four times. He went to Notts County, Doncaster Rovers (twice) and Northampton Town in an effort to rack up games and also to put himself on the radar of English clubs. He knew that his days at Villa were over.

When it ended there wasn't a big fuss made. There were no tears in the first-team changing room or angry rants about the club letting a talented player go. It was a quiet exit as Stevens dropped three divisions to join Portsmouth in League Two. So long to the Premier League!

***

The ambition was to return to the Premier League and the journey began with a cramp-inducing hike through a forest.

Pre-season is not meant to be an easy period. It is when players build muscle strength, add endurance and load up on fitness levels to ensure that their body is fully equipped for the long season ahead. Some teams make it a little more adventurous, though.

For the Portsmouth players in the summer of 2015, the football almost became an aspirational object, like the Holy Grail, that the players one day might be lucky enough to get a sight of. At least that is how it felt as they trekked through a forest in leg-burning runs and stomach-turning ascents that made sure the last of the cocktails from a summer holiday came back up, albeit in a different combination of colour and texture.

Pushing players to their limits is what Paul Cook does. He believes in the discipline that hard work embeds into someone's soul. He sees merit in the break-them-down-to-build-them-up approach. Most of all, he maintains that something is not worth doing unless it's done right.

The former Sligo Rovers manager was fully aware of Stevens's qualities from his time in the League of Ireland. He was also aware of the improvements that the left-sided defender needed to make to his game.

Stevens tells the story: 'When I went down to League Two, that was probably the first time I was ever coached properly. It was the first time that I was coached to actually play my position. That helped me go from strength to strength and learn the game more and more. I wasn't really coached at Aston Villa.

'At Villa you had players who knew the game inside out, there were big names there, big players who probably didn't need the coaching. But I did need it, more so than anybody else. I was only there for one and a half seasons. I spent the rest of the time out on loan. It might have been a different story if Alex McLeish had stayed in charge, because he signed me. When I went back for that pre-season I was in the best nick that I could be in … I did a lot of training with Philly McMahon in Ireland, so I gave myself every chance. But it didn't happen for me and I felt that I needed that bit of help to get up to speed in the Premier League.

'I just think Cookie [Paul Cook] understood me as a person and knew how to find my edge. He finds that with all of his players. He did a lot of coaching on [team] shape, how he wanted us to set up, how he wanted us to play, how he wanted us to defend. He backed me to play well. He'd pull you in, he would hammer you, he would slaughter you, but he would show you exactly what you were doing wrong and what you should be doing right.

Those were the things that I didn't really get in the Premier League and that is when I probably would've needed it the most. Looking back, I was not to know if I was good enough at the time. But [if] I was my League Two self in the Premier League [with Villa] I would've stood a better chance.'

Perhaps Premier League teams simply do not have the time to coach the basics to a player they recruit for their first-team squad. Or maybe the type of coaching expertise that outsiders expect to exist at the top level of English football is not really there.

But every industry must constantly adapt. Sure, even the Church is ditching the sharing basket for Revolut. So coaches have no excuses any more. There is always a way to be a better coach. And players who receive better coaching will ultimately fulfil their potential.

The potential was always clear to see in Stevens. It is why Villa signed him in the first place and it is why former Republic of Ireland manager Giovanni Trapattoni quizzed Ciaran Clark about his club-mate when he was in the Premier League for the first time. Yet Stevens needed to learn a lot more before he was truly ready. He took inspiration from fellow Irishman Michael Doyle, who was a senior pro at Portsmouth. He was always at the front in running sessions, always first on the training pitch and always treated each day as if he were fighting for a new contract. It was how a professional footballer should be.

Between Cook's coaching, Doyle's leadership and a new-found desire to return to the top, Stevens set about adding the two key components that had been missing from his game: consistency and improved decision-making.

Obviously it paid off as, after two impressive seasons at Portsmouth, the upwardly mobile Sheffield United bid for him in 2017. He didn't know it yet, but he was on his way back to the Premier League with the Blades. Stevens would play a key role in their eventual promotion.

'It was a great feeling because I felt more part of it. I wasn't on the outside, maybe getting in [to the side] and going back out. I was there, I was a mainstay and I'm actually going to have an opportunity to play here.

It was like a first chance [to play in the Premier League]. Obviously with Villa the manager gave me an unbelievable opportunity to play in it but I was ready with Sheff U for it. It was just a fact that I had every box ticked. I had my fitness, my confidence, my consistency. Now it just came down to ability. If you're good enough, you're good enough. And thankfully that season we were good enough.'

Sheffield United's first season in the Premier League was a runaway success. 'We had a unique way of playing that year and not many teams would have experienced it. We never changed our mentality or the way that we were going to play. We obviously knew who we were coming up against but we didn't fear teams, we respected them. We had that belief that we could win the game. It was a good first season. We had massive togetherness in the changing room. If we played bad, we all played bad together. I remember we went to Goodison Park to play Everton and got absolutely battered but we ended up winning 2-0. We all dug in deep for each other. You're doing it with lads who you would run through a brick wall for.'

A ninth-place finish in the 2019–20 season for Sheffield United was fully deserved. So too were the plaudits that flowed in for Stevens, who played thirty-eight games, scored two goals and became a regular with Ireland at international level.

However, second season syndrome hit hard, with the club tumbling down the table before being relegated following a campaign that was blighted by injuries, bad luck and an absence of crowds due to the COVID-19 outbreak.

Stevens explains: 'I think a lot of things cost us in our second season. We lost the fans due to COVID and that was a new experience for everybody. We were a team that needed fans in the stadium to create an atmosphere. We had a lot of injuries and it was such a short turnaround from the first season – it was probably the shortest pre-season that we could've had, our squad was slim and we never reached the level of performance from the first season.

'For me, I started in the Premier League when I came over to England and then had to wait so many years to get back there. So you have to take the opportunity when it comes around. You want to be playing in the Premier League, especially after you've had a taste of it, you want more of it.'

The ambition was to prove that he was capable of performing consistently in the Premier League. Stevens did just that.

30
Andrew Omobamidele

Norwich City (2021–22)
Games Played: 5
Goals Scored: 1
Assists Created: 0
Clean Sheets: 0
Yellow Cards: 1
Red Cards: 0
Wins: 1
Draws: 0
Losses: 4

It's Arsenal away. Three-time English Premier League champions. Record winners of the FA Cup. The eleventh richest club in the world. It's the Emirates Stadium. Over 60,000 spectators, mostly clad in red and white. An amphitheatre where gladiators show little to no respect to smaller opponents.

Norwich City are on a losing streak. Three games played, ten goals conceded. Manager Daniel Farke is addressing his players in the function room of a London hotel. He chooses his words wisely, knowing that his best will be required a few hours later before his team leave their dressing room.

As Farke paces across the front of the room, a squad of players sit and watch his every action, knowing that he is about to reveal the starting line-up. The manager presses a sheet of paper onto a tactics board and players either exhale with a sense of relief or look down at the ground in anger.

'Tim Krul,' begins Farke as he reads the team line-up aloud. 'Max Aarons on the right, Brandon Williams on the left, Grant Hanley and Andrew Omobamidele at centre-back.'

Okay, stop, did he just say that Number 44, that nineteen-year-old kid, is going to start? Away to Arsenal? In the Premier League?

Except Omobamidele isn't overly surprised. Sure, he is a little taken aback but this is someone who, in his own words, 'sets my goals as high as I can so that whatever I achieve there is still more to aim for'. He has also just made his Republic of Ireland senior debut ten days previously. If ever there was a time to believe in himself it is now.

The meeting breaks up and the players retreat to their rooms. Omobamidele is finally alone with his thoughts. He sits on the edge of the bed, reaches for his mobile phone, presses on the message app and begins typing. This is a moment that he has dreamed about since he was a little boy: telling the world that he is about to make his Premier League debut.

He types the simplest of messages: 'I'm starting', and presses send. He then switches his phone off, before he is tempted to reveal the news to anyone else. One single message sent to Kenny Molloy, the first coach that Omobamidele had as a nine-year-old at Leixlip United. 'If I text my mam she probably would have blown up my phone [with calls and messages],' laughs Omobamidele as he recalls his attempts to avoid the hype before that first Premier League game.

Typical of his laid-back demeanour and steely focus on the task at hand, Omobamidele did not seek the extra attention. He would deal with all of that later on. He had business to contend with and that involved helping

Norwich to possibly upset one of the league's top teams. Oh, and he had to man-mark one of its most deadly finishers in Pierre-Emerick Aubameyang. 'Bring it on' was all that he could think.

Of course, the commentators reporting on the game suddenly had a problem. How do you pronounce the debutant's name? OMO-BAM-E-DELE. And again? OMO-BAM-E-DELE. Perfect! An Irish kid with African heritage on his father's side, he laughs now when he hears people get tongue-tied, but there's also a sense of pride that he is representing his family and bringing their name onto the world stage.

In fact, it was when he played his first-ever game in front of TV cameras that people began to mutter his name, talk about his potential to do great things in the world of professional football. This was a world away from the Premier League, his competitive debut for the Ireland Under-17s at the UEFA Under-17 European Championships in 2019. It gave him a platform to showcase his ability. 'I was late coming into the Under-17s. We had a couple of games out in Marbella. I came on as a sub against Poland and then I started against Belgium … I can't remember the score but I do remember that I scored in the game. That was in February and then the finals was in May, so I was very much a latecomer to the group,' says Omobamidele.

'The management and the players had already been together for the guts of a year, but when I got the call-up I didn't just want to make up the numbers, I wanted to play. I think I'm used to being someone who has to prove themselves and I don't mind that at all. Actually I kind of like setting my expectations high. It's something that my old coach, Kenny Molloy, instilled into me. Even when I went in at Norwich, I knew that I was the young lad being asked to train with the first team, but after two or three matches I wanted to push on and play. That was the same thing that happened with the Under-17s. It's a mentality thing. Football is a team sport but everyone is fighting for their jersey … if I'm starting there is going to be two or three players behind me that want my jersey, so you always have to keep striving for more. Even if I'm on the bench, I'm looking at the player ahead of me and wondering why are they ahead of me. So I have to learn from them to add to my game and work on the things that I need to play at the level that I want to be at.'

Mentality is just one component required to become a Premier League footballer. However, Norwich City knew that Omobamidele possessed other attributes, due to his putting them on full display at the Under-17 Euros tournament in Ireland, where he played in the three Group A games that the home nation featured in – draws with Greece, the Czech Republic and Belgium.

As the RTÉ and Eurosport cameras beamed out live coverage of the games, viewers were able to see just why Omobamidele was standing out. Combined with a 6ft 2in frame, muscular build, athletic stride and powerful jump was an assured short passing game, ability to anticipate danger and frightening recovery speed. Oh, and he was a threat in both penalty areas, as he proved by scoring an eighty-eighth-minute equaliser against the Czech Republic.

Ireland's adventure in that tournament did not extend beyond the group stage, but Omobamidele simply swapped one rollercoaster for another as he joined Norwich for pre-season. The club's plan was for the Kildare youngster to spend time developing in their Under-18 team, adapt to living away from home and see how he progressed. Within a couple of months, however, he was dominating in their Under-23 side and a first-team debut was inevitable – eventually coming in January 2021.

'Norwich were still in the Championship when I made my debut. The boys had done such a great job in the first part of the season, but I got my chance and played ten games in that season. So when I went into the next pre-season I was still on a high. Obviously the Premier League is a whole different ball game but I still wanted to keep up what I was doing,' says Omobamidele.

Learning from the leaders around him is a trait that he developed as a child. Whether it was his parents or coaches, he has always viewed information as a power source that gives him extra strength and confidence. So it's hardly surprising that he is acting like a sponge at his club, soaking in as much information as his experienced team-mates are willing to share. 'Tim Krul is someone who I pick up a lot from. He's been in the game a long time and he's a great professional. Even when I came in in the Championship, he was always giving me little pointers, even off the pitch I've picked up a lot from him,' he states.

Interestingly, at the time of speaking with Omobamidele, he has just moved into a new house; his first house. The newly painted rooms feel empty and almost too big for a young man to occupy on his own. But this is part of the process of growing up, of becoming a Premier League player. He's no longer a kid who the club needs to check in on, he's now a man who must take care of himself. With that comes extra responsibility. Pay the mortgage. Clear the bills. Do the weekly shopping. Enhance the cooking skills. Put the bins out. The mundane cost of living in the modern world.

Of course there is a risk factor that comes with buying your own home, but taking risk is part of his DNA. Perhaps he spent too much time watching his idol Rio Ferdinand, who was among the first Premier League centre-backs to be daring enough to carry the ball out of defence or to attempt a long pass that could either spark an attack or put his own team immediately on the back foot. Omobamidele is the same; he wants the ball at his feet and is willing to take a gamble.

The important thing, however, is that he is learning when to do those things. He explains that there was more room for error when playing in the Championship but the elevation to the Premier League has taught him that every decision he makes on the pitch has an impact on the game.

'[Playing in the Premier League] has made me have a better understanding of the game because the level is so high. I read the game better, I feel, and I know the best moments to step in to break a line with the ball or the best moment or time in the game to pass a ball through the line,' he explains. 'When you go into the Premier League, the standards go up. When I was first on the bench you're watching games live in front of you so you see how a centre-back plays. I always try to nit-pick bits out of their game that I can bring into mine. So that has helped to understand when to do or not to do certain things.

'When I was growing up I looked at Rio Ferdinand a lot. But I watch football differently now. Before I would just watch the game, now I'm watching the positions that the centre-backs take up. Like if a ball is getting whipped in, I'll be looking at the two centre-backs instead of the ball. Those centre-backs are playing there for a reason and that is the level that I want to be at, playing week in, week out in the best league in the world. Picking up on all of those little details, because that is what separates the average centre-backs from the good ones.'

It's clear that Omobamidele is a deep thinker on the game. 'Football has evolved and it is more building up through the thirds. Obviously your first job as a centre-back is to defend but it helps if one of your centre-backs can start the play. Finding that balance between the centre-backs is key, but it all depends on how the manager wants you to play. I like to play out from the back, but I'm very much someone who loves defending. The strikers and attackers are there for a reason but I'm happy to be a defender.'

He wasn't always a centre-back; he actually started out as a forward in schoolboy football. He jokes that his attacking instincts haven't completely disappeared when the topic of his first Premier League goal away to Leeds United comes up. A thumping header in a 2-1 loss. Never mind Rio Ferdinand, he could have been the next Didier Drogba. He laughs and brushes it off as just another way to help his team.

The knack of taking such achievements in his stride is admirable yet also expected at Premier League level. Forget about seeking likes and flattering comments on social media, he wants the approval of his manager and acceptance of his team-mates. And that is exactly why making his debut and scoring his first goal in the Premier League did not properly 'sink in for a few days'. He was so focused on the task at hand that he almost forgot what he had just done – on both occasions.

'I think I'm at my best when I know what I'm doing for the next week or the week after or even the next month. I have the same routine every week and pretty much every weekend, really. Whether that is having some close friends come over to chill or playing PlayStation, but my advice for anybody is that you need a good routine,' says Omobamidele. 'The consistency is important. I'm always trying to improve – like cooking, for example. I think I'm in between [being a] simple cook and good cook. Another big part of my routine is sleep. I've learned that it is so important to get the right amount of sleep in to recover and to make sure that you are fully rested.'

The discipline that Omobamidele has instilled into his everyday life away from the pitch has now been matched by a growing desire to be the best that he can on the pitch. An injury to his lower back in December 2021 halted that pursuit, however, just when he was beginning to build some momentum.

Rather than book the first flight to Dubai for an extended holiday or wallow in self-pity, the Kildare native got to work: studying himself. He knocked on the door of Norwich's Performance Analysis Department to seek footage of his games so that he could identify patterns in his own play – how he ran, how he covered space, how he linked up with his fellow centre-back, when he moved forward, what sort of passes he made, how closely he marked an opposition striker, etc.

'I've kind of taken it as if there is nothing that I can do about my injury now. Of course I'm doing the rehab and everything that goes with that, but I'm using the time to see if I can improve on other sides of the game,' reveals Omobamidele. 'It's more on the analysis side of things. I've been watching back the Arsenal game, the Leeds game, just to see if there are things that I can improve on. It's trying to see things from a different angle, even from a coach's angle. As I said before, I'm watching other centre-backs all of the time but lately I've been comparing what I do in certain situations to what they do. Now that I have time to study all of that, hopefully it will make me a better player when I get back onto the pitch.

'If you are playing and then when you watch a clip after a game you don't look at that clip the same way as you would when you are injured and looking at it. You are more unbiased compared to when you are playing. I look at it more through a ruthless lens and I ask the coaches for feedback, because when I get back I want to know what exactly I have to do and what I have to improve on. The biggest thing is knowledge; knowing how to play the game. It can be a simple game then it's not at the same time. For me, I want to widen my knowledge base and become the best player that I can be.'

In many ways Omobamidele typifies the modern-day footballer with an almost robotic approach to maintaining a routine, an openness to learning and absorbing critical analysis, plus an ability to combine natural talent and fine-tuned athleticism with an acute understanding of the game. Add to that a level of temperament that handles pressure with ease and a personality that keeps him humble yet ambitious at the same time. He is what the Premier League demands of a young player.

And you will not catch Omobamidele slacking. He has a support base of family and friends to keep him grounded, while regular visits back to where it all began at Leixlip United remind him of when he was just another boy with a dream of playing in the Premier League.

Now that that dream has become his reality expect Omobamidele to make the most of it.

Statistics

Most Appearances

451 – Shay Given
445 – John O'Shea
431 – Richard Dunne
392 – Damien Duff
377 – Stephen Carr
366 – Roy Keane
359 – Rory Delap
349 – Robbie Keane
344 – Shane Long
335 – Kenny Cunningham

Most Goals

126 – Robbie Keane
59 – Niall Quinn
56 – Shane Long
54 – Damien Duff
43 – Jonathan Walters
39 – Roy Keane
37 – Kevin Doyle
28 – Ian Harte
23 – Rory Delap
21 – Seamus Coleman/Stephen Hunt

Most Assists

55 – Damien Duff
39 – Robbie Keane
37 – Niall Quinn
36 – Ian Harte
33 – Roy Keane
31 – Gary Kelly
30 – Andy Townsend
28 – Stephen Ireland/Steve Staunton
25 – Denis Irwin

Most Clean Sheets

(for a goalkeeper)

113 – Shay Given
54 – Dean Kiely
18 – Alan Kelly
15 – Keith Branagan/Paddy Kenny
8 – Robert Elliot
7 – Darren Randolph
2 – Caoimhín Kelleher
1 – Mark Travers/Keiren Westwood

Most Appearances as a Substitute

158 – Shane Long
77 – Stephen Ireland
76 – Robbie Keane
75 – John O'Shea
65 – Damien Duff
59 – James McClean
53 – Robbie Brady
50 – Kevin Kilbane/Niall Quinn
44 – Jonathan Walters

Most Yellow Cards

74 – Richard Dunne
69 – Roy Keane
54 – Stephen Carr
52 – Ciaran Clark
48 – James McCarthy
47 – Lee Carsley
46 – Rory Delap
44 – Glenn Whelan
40 – Andy Townsend
36 – Gary Kelly

Most Red Cards

8 – Richard Dunne
7 – Roy Keane
4 – Rory Delap
3 – Ciaran Clark/Kevin Kilbane/Steve Staunton/Andy Townsend
2 – Gary Breen/Stephen Carr/Seamus Coleman/Kenny Cunningham/John Egan/Jeff Hendrick/Robbie Keane/Gary Kelly/David Meyler/Andy O'Brien/Marc Wilson

Most Wins

220 – Roy Keane
218 – John O'Shea
185 – Denis Irwin
168 – Shay Given
150 – Damien Duff
139 – Robbie Keane
136 – Richard Dunne
133 – Seamus Coleman
131 – Gary Kelly
119 – Steve Staunton

Most Draws

127 – Shay Given
120 – Richard Dunne
106 – Stephen Carr
105 – John O'Shea
103 – Rory Delap
101 – Damien Duff
98 – Kenny Cunningham
93 – Seamus Coleman
88 – Robbie Keane
86 – Denis Irwin

Most Losses

175 – Richard Dunne
156 – Shay Given
155 – Stephen Carr
150 – Rory Delap/Shane Long
149 – Kevin Kilbane

141 – Damien Duff

136 – Kenny Cunningham

122 – Robbie Keane/John O'Shea

Youngest Debutants

17 years 28 days – Stephen Carr (Tottenham Hotspur v Ipswich Town, 26/9/1993)

17 years 112 days – Richard Dunne (Everton v Sheffield Wednesday, 11/1/1997)

17 years 123 days – Evan Ferguson (Brighton & Hove Albion v Burnley, 19/2/2022)

17 years 145 days – Andy Turner (Tottenham Hotspur v Southampton, 15/8/1992)

17 years 179 days – Alan Maybury (Leeds United v Aston Villa, 3/2/1996)

17 years 199 days – Michael Obafemi (Southampton v Tottenham Hotspur, 21/1/2018)

17 years 268 days – Willie Boland (Coventry City v Chelsea, 1/5/1993)

17 years 306 days – Troy Parrott (Tottenham Hotspur v Burnley, 7/12/2019)

17 years 333 days – Aaron Doran (Blackburn Rovers v Liverpool, 11/4/2009)

18 years 0 days – Leon Best (Southampton v Newcastle United, 19/9/2004)

Oldest Players

40 years 151 days – Shay Given (Stoke City v Crystal Palace, 18/9/2016)

38 years 226 days – Dean Kiely (West Bromwich Albion v Blackburn Rovers, 24/5/2009)

38 years 197 days – Denis Irwin (Wolverhampton Wanderers v Tottenham Hotspur, 15/5/2004)

38 years 8 days – Kevin Moran (Blackburn Rovers v Ipswich Town, 7/5/1994)

37 years 158 days – Paul McGrath (Derby County v Arsenal, 11/5/1997)

36 years 255 days – Gerry Peyton (Chelsea v Sheffield Wednesday, 30/1/1993)

36 years 220 days – Damien Delaney (Crystal Palace v Tottenham Hotspur, 25/2/2018)

36 years 62 days – Lee Carsley (Birmingham City v Burnley, 1/5/2010)

36 years 43 days – Rory Delap (Stoke City v Reading, 18/8/2012)

36 years 36 days – Andy Townsend (Middlesbrough v Aston Villa, 28/8/1999)

Youngest Goalscorers

17 years 166 days – Andy Turner (Tottenham Hotspur v Everton, 5/9/1992)

18 years 169 days – Michael Obafemi (Southampton v Huddersfield Town, 22/12/2018)

18 years 251 days – Damien Duff (Blackburn Rovers v Everton, 8/11/1997)

18 years 352 days – Ian Harte (Leeds United v Derby County, 17/8/1996)

18 years 361 days – Clinton Morrison (Crystal Palace v Sheffield Wednesday, 10/5/1998)

19 years 44 days – Robbie Keane (Coventry City v Derby County, 21/8/1999)

19 years 65 days – James McCarthy (Wigan Athletic v Wolverhampton Wanderers, 16/1/2010)

19 years 129 days – Anthony Stokes (Sunderland v Derby County, 1/12/2007)

19 years 130 days – Andrew Omobamidele (Norwich City v Leeds United, 31/10/2021)

19 years 205 days – Willo Flood (Manchester City v Norwich City, 1/11/2004)

Oldest Goalscorers

37 years 114 days – Kevin Moran (Blackburn Rovers v Oldham Athletic, 21/8/1993)

36 years 135 days – Paul McGrath (Aston Villa v West Ham United, 17/4/1996)

35 years 143 days – Rory Delap (Stoke City v Blackburn Rovers, 26/11/2011)

35 years 136 days – Andy Townsend (Middlesbrough v Newcastle United, 6/12/1998)

35 years 126 days – Niall Quinn (Sunderland v Derby County, 9/2/2002)

35 years 28 days – Shane Long (Southampton v Everton, 19/2/2022)

34 years 257 days – Damien Delaney (Crystal Palace v West Ham United, 2/4/2016)

34 years 153 days – Denis Irwin (Manchester United v West Ham United, 1/4/2000)

33 years 269 days – Wes Hoolahan (Norwich City v West Ham United, 13/2/2016)

33 years 248 days – Lee Carsley (Everton v Birmingham City, 3/11/2007)

Premier League Winners

7 – Denis Irwin, Roy Keane (Manchester United)

5 – John O'Shea (Manchester United)

2 – Damien Duff (Chelsea)

1 – Darron Gibson (Manchester United), Jeff Kenna (Blackburn Rovers)

Player Of The Month

April 1997: Mickey Evans (Southampton)

October 1998: Roy Keane (Manchester United)

August 1999: Robbie Keane (Coventry City)

December 1999: Roy Keane (Manchester United)

January 2001: Robbie Keane (Leeds United)

April 2007: Robbie Keane (Tottenham Hotspur)

PFA Players' Player of the Year

1992/93: Paul McGrath (Aston Villa)

1999/2000: Roy Keane (Manchester United)

PFA Team of The Year

1992/93: Paul McGrath (Aston Villa), Roy Keane (Nottingham Forest)

1993/94: Gary Kelly (Leeds United), Denis Irwin (Manchester United)

1996/97: Roy Keane (Manchester United)

1998/99: Denis Irwin (Manchester United)

1999/2000: Gary Kelly (Leeds United), Ian Harte (Leeds United), Roy Keane (Manchester United)

2000/01: Stephen Carr (Tottenham Hotspur), Roy Keane (Manchester United)

2001/02: Steve Finnan (Fulham), Shay Given (Newcastle United), Roy Keane (Manchester United)

2002/03: Stephen Carr (Tottenham Hotspur)

2005/06: Shay Given (Newcastle United)

2009/10: Richard Dunne (Aston Villa)

2013/14: Seamus Coleman (Everton)

Full List of Irish Premier League Players

1. Keith Andrews (Wolverhampton Wanderers, Blackburn Rovers, West Bromwich Albion)
2. Harry Arter (Bournemouth, Cardiff City)
3. Phil Babb (Coventry City, Liverpool, Sunderland)
4. Steve Baker (Middlesbrough)
5. Graham Barrett (Arsenal)
6. Leon Best (Southampton, Newcastle United)
7. Willie Boland (Coventry City)
8. Danny Boxall (Crystal Palace)
9. Lee Boylan (West Ham United)
10. Robbie Brady (Hull City, Norwich City, Burnley)
11. Keith Branagan (Bolton Wanderers, Ipswich Town)
12. Gary Breen (Coventry City, West Ham United, Sunderland)
13. Alex Bruce (Birmingham City, Hull City)
14. Paul Butler (Sunderland, Wolverhampton Wanderers)
15. Thomas Butler (Sunderland)
16. Shaun Byrne (West Ham United)
17. Brian Carey (Leicester City)
18. Stephen Carr (Tottenham Hotspur, Newcastle United, Birmingham City)
19. Samir Carruthers (Aston Villa)
20. Lee Carsley (Derby County, Blackburn Rovers, Coventry City, Everton, Birmingham City)
21. Tony Cascarino (Chelsea)
22. Cyrus Christie (Fulham)
23. Ciaran Clark (Aston Villa, Newcastle United)
24. Clive Clarke (West Ham United)
25. Seamus Coleman (Everton)
26. Nick Colgan (Chelsea)
27. Nathan Collins (Burnley)
28. Aaron Connolly (Brighton & Hove Albion)
29. David Connolly (Wigan Athletic, Sunderland)

30. Simon Cox (West Bromwich Albion)
31. Owen Coyle (Bolton Wanderers)
32. Jim Crawford (Newcastle United)
33. Josh Cullen (West Ham United)
34. Michael Cummins (Middlesbrough)
35. Greg Cunningham (Manchester City, Cardiff City)
36. Kenny Cunningham (Wimbledon, Birmingham City)
37. Liam Daish (Coventry City)
38. Damien Delaney (Leicester City, Crystal Palace)
39. Rory Delap (Derby County, Southampton, Sunderland, Stoke City)
40. Gary Doherty (Tottenham Hotspur, Norwich City)
41. Matt Doherty (Wolverhampton Wanderers, Tottenham Hotspur)
42. Aaron Doran (Blackburn Rovers)
43. Jonathan Douglas (Blackburn Rovers)
44. Colin Doyle (Birmingham City)
45. Kevin Doyle (Reading, Wolverhampton Wanderers, Crystal Palace)
46. Damien Duff (Blackburn Rovers, Chelsea, Newcastle United, Fulham)
47. Shane Duffy (Everton, Brighton & Hove Albion)
48. Jimmy Dunne (Burnley)
49. Richard Dunne (Everton, Manchester City, Aston Villa, QPR)
50. John Egan (Sheffield United)
51. Rob Elliot (Newcastle United)
52. Stephen Elliott (Manchester City, Sunderland)
53. Mickey Evans (Southampton)
54. Keith Fahey (Birmingham City)
55. Gareth Farrelly (Aston Villa, Everton, Bolton Wanderers)
56. Neale Fenn (Tottenham Hotspur)
57. Evan Ferguson (Brighton & Hove Albion)
58. Steve Finnan (Fulham, Liverpool, Portsmouth)
59. Scott Fitzgerald (Wimbledon)
60. Curtis Fleming (Middlesbrough)
61. Willo Flood (Manchester City)

62.   Caleb Folan (Wigan Athletic, Hull City)

63.   Tony Folan (Crystal Palace)

64.   Dominic Foley (Watford)

65.   Kevin Foley (Wolverhampton Wanderers)

66.   Anthony Forde (Wolverhampton Wanderers)

67.   Owen Garvan (Crystal Palace)

68.   Jason Gavin (Middlesbrough)

69.   Derek Geary (Sheffield United)

70.   Darron Gibson (Manchester United, Everton, Sunderland)

71.   Rory Ginty (Crystal Palace)

72.   Shay Given (Blackburn Rovers, Newcastle United, Manchester City, Aston Villa, Stoke City)

73.   Jon Goodman (Wimbledon)

74.   Jack Grealish (Aston Villa)

75.   Reece Grego-Cox (QPR)

76.   Michael Harriman (QPR)

77.   Ian Harte (Leeds United, Sunderland, Reading)

78.   Jeff Hendrick (Burnley)

79.   Matt Holland (Ipswich Town, Charlton Athletic)

80.   Wes Hoolahan (Norwich City)

81.   Ray Houghton (Aston Villa, Crystal Palace)

82.   Conor Hourihane (Aston Villa)

83.   Noel Hunt (Reading)

84.   Stephen Hunt (Reading, Hull City, Wolverhampton Wanderers)

85.   Adam Idah (Norwich City)

86.   Stephen Ireland (Manchester City, Aston Villa, Newcastle United, Stoke City)

87.   Denis Irwin (Manchester United, Wolverhampton Wanderers)

88.   Graham Kavanagh (Middlesbrough, Wigan Athletic)

89.   Robbie Keane (Coventry City, Leeds United, Tottenham Hotspur, Liverpool, West Ham United, Aston Villa)

90.   Roy Keane (Nottingham Forest, Manchester United)

91.   Caoimhín Kelleher (Liverpool)

92.   Alan Kelly (Sheffield United, Blackburn Rovers)

93.   David Kelly (Sunderland)

94.   Gary Kelly (Leeds United)

95.   Stephen Kelly (Tottenham Hotspur, Birmingham City, Stoke City, Fulham, Reading)

96.   Jeff Kenna (Southampton, Blackburn Rovers, Birmingham City)

97.   Mark Kennedy (Liverpool, Wimbledon, Manchester City, Wolverhampton Wanderers)

98.   Paddy Kenny (Sheffield United, QPR)

99.   Andy Keogh (Wolverhampton Wanderers)

100.   Alan Kernaghan (Middlesbrough, Manchester City)

101.   Dean Kiely (Charlton Athletic, Portsmouth, West Bromwich Albion)

102.   Kevin Kilbane (Sunderland, Everton, Wigan Athletic, Hull City)

103.   Mark Kinsella (Charlton Athletic, Aston Villa)

104.   Brian Launders (Arsenal)

105.   Liam Lawrence (Sunderland, Stoke City)

106.   Kevin Long (Burnley)

107.   Shane Long (Reading, West Bromwich Albion, Hull City, Southampton)

108.   Jon Macken (Manchester City, Derby County)

109.   Alan Mahon (Blackburn Rovers, Wigan Athletic)

110.   Alan Maybury (Leeds United)

111.   Jason McAteer (Bolton Wanderers, Liverpool, Blackburn Rovers, Sunderland)

112.   Chris McCann (Burnley)

113.   James McCarthy (Wigan Athletic, Everton, Crystal Palace)

114.   Paddy McCarthy (Crystal Palace)

115.   Sean McCarthy (Oldham Athletic)

116.   James McClean (Sunderland, West Bromwich Albion)

117.   David McDonald (Tottenham Hotspur)

118.   Aiden McGeady (Everton)

119.   Paul McGee (Wimbledon)

120.   David McGoldrick (Sheffield United)

121. Eddie McGoldrick (Crystal Palace, Arsenal)

122. Brian McGovern (Arsenal)

123. John McGrath (Aston Villa)

124. Paul McGrath (Aston Villa, Derby County)

125. Mark McKeever (Sheffield United)

126. Stephen McPhail (Leeds United)

127. Paul McShane (Sunderland, Hull City)

128. David Meyler (Sunderland, Hull City)

129. Liam Miller (Manchester United, Sunderland)

130. Mike Milligan (Oldham Athletic, Norwich City)

131. Jayson Molumby (Brighton & Hove Albion)

132. Alan Moore (Middlesbrough)

133. Kevin Moran (Blackburn Rovers)

134. Chris Morris (Middlesbrough)

135. Clinton Morrison (Crystal Palace, Birmingham City)

136. Daryl Murphy (Sunderland)

137. Joe Murphy (West Bromwich Albion)

138. Michael Obafemi (Southampton)

139. Alan O'Brien (Newcastle United)

140. Andy O'Brien (Bradford City, Newcastle United, Portsmouth, Bolton Wanderers)

141. Joey O'Brien (Bolton Wanderers, West Ham United)

142. Liam O'Brien (Newcastle United)

143. Roy O'Donovan (Sunderland)

144. Keith O'Halloran (Middlesbrough)

145. Eunan O'Kane (Bournemouth)

146. David O'Leary (Arsenal, Leeds United)

147. Keith O'Neill (Norwich City, Middlesbrough)

148. Dara O'Shea (West Bromwich Albion)

149. Jay O'Shea (Birmingham City)

150. John O'Shea (Manchester United, Sunderland)

151. Andrew Omobamidele (Norwich City)

152. Marcos Painter (Birmingham City)

153. Troy Parrott (Tottenham Hotspur)
154. Alex Pearce (Reading)
155. Gerry Peyton (Chelsea)
156. Terry Phelan (Manchester City, Chelsea, Everton)
157. Anthony Pilkington (Norwich City)
158. Darren Potter (Liverpool)
159. Lee Power (Norwich City)
160. Alan Quinn (Sheffield Wednesday, Sheffield United)
161. Barry Quinn (Coventry City)
162. Niall Quinn (Manchester City, Sunderland)
163. Rob Quinn (Crystal Palace)
164. Stephen Quinn (Sheffield United, Hull City)
165. Darren Randolph (Charlton Athletic, West Ham United)
166. Michael Reddy (Sunderland)
167. Andy Reid (Tottenham Hotspur, Charlton Athletic, Sunderland, Blackpool)
168. Steven Reid (Blackburn Rovers, West Bromwich Albion, Burnley)
169. Declan Rice (West Ham United)
170. Callum Robinson (Aston Villa, Sheffield United)
171. Matthew Rush (West Ham United)
172. Richie Ryan (Sunderland)
173. Conor Sammon (Wigan Athletic)
174. John Sheridan (Sheffield Wednesday, Bolton Wanderers)
175. Tony Sheridan (Coventry City)
176. Bernie Slaven (Middlesbrough)
177. Will Smallbone (Southampton)
178. Tony Springett (Norwich City)
179. Steve Staunton (Aston Villa, Liverpool)
180. Enda Stevens (Aston Villa, Sheffield United)
181. Anthony Stokes (Sunderland)
182. Jay Tabb (Reading)
183. Sean Thornton (Sunderland)
184. Kevin Toner (Aston Villa)

185.   Andy Townsend (Chelsea, Aston Villa, Middlesbrough)

186.   Mark Travers (Bournemouth)

187.   Keith Treacy (Blackburn Rovers)

188.   Andy Turner (Tottenham Hotspur)

189.   Jonathan Walters (Bolton Wanderers, Stoke City, Burnley)

190.   Stephen Ward (Wolverhampton Wanderers, Burnley)

191.   Keiren Westwood (Sunderland)

192.   Gareth Whalley (Bradford City)

193.   Glenn Whelan (Stoke City)

194.   Ronnie Whelan (Liverpool)

195.   Derrick Williams (Aston Villa)

196.   Marc Wilson (Portsmouth, Stoke City, Bournemouth, West Bromwich Albion)

197.   Mark Yeates (Tottenham Hotspur)

Alex Bruce, Jack Grealish and Declan Rice switched international allegiances after making their Premier League debuts
**Kevin Gallen, Will Keane and Richard Stearman declared for Ireland after making their Premier League debuts*
***No Irish players have appeared for Brentford, Huddersfield Town or Swindon Town in the Premier League*

Thanks to Neil O'Riordan, Stephen Finn and Joe McCarthy for fact-checking.

Acknowledgements

Writing about the English Premier League, through the perspective of Irish players, is something that I had long wanted to do. The League's thirtieth anniversary gave me the perfect reason to finally do just that.

It is important to acknowledge that Irish footballers were thriving in English football long before the Premier League came along. So this book is not intended to overlook their achievements but to focus on the players who have been part of the first three decades of a League that has become the richest and most popular in world sport.

This book is not about the thirty best Irish players to play in that League; it is about the unique experiences of thirty Irishmen who each have a different story to tell. I'm incredibly grateful to each of them for allowing me to peer into their world and attempt to capture what made their association with the Premier League so fascinating.

Thank you to everyone at New Island Books for believing in this project and bringing it to the book shelves (and electronic tablets), especially Stephen Reid and editor Noel O'Regan.

Finally, thank you to my parents and my brother, who have always been my greatest supporters.

Many Thanks,
Gareth

Index